TANKS AND ARMORED VEHICLES

Bruce LaFontaine

DOVER PUBLICATIONS, INC.
Mineola, New York

Bibliographical Note

Tanks and Armored Vehicles is a new work, first published by Dover Publications, Inc., in 2000.

International Standard Book Number
ISBN-13: 978-0-486-41317-4
ISBN-10: 0-486-41317-9

Manufactured in the United States by LSC Communications
41317913   2019
www.doverpublications.com

INTRODUCTION

The development of the armored combat tank was driven by the brutal trench warfare battles of World War I. By 1915, the armies in this conflict had settled into a stalemate comprised of miles of opposing trenches, barbed wire fences, and fortified machine gun emplacements. Behind the trench lines were massed battalions of artillery able to rain down cannon-fire on the entrenched soldiers. The area between the opposing trenches was called "No Man's Land." Each side would attack and counterattack across this killing zone with neither side able to gain a tactical or strategic advantage. Thousands of soldiers died in these desperate and bloody attempts to overwhelm the enemy positions.

A new weapon was needed to break this cycle of futile battles: a vehicle that could cross No Man's Land, break through the enemy barrier, and achieve a crucial victory. Such a machine would need to be armored to withstand rifle fire, machines guns, and hand grenades. It would have to traverse muddy battlefields covered with foxholes and large artillery shell craters. The British army was the first to investigate and develop an armored track-driven vehicle with these capabilities. They tested a number of agricultural tractors with continuous loop tracks. Based on the success of these trials, Britain produced the first armored, track-driven demonstration vehicle, nicknamed *Little Willie*. It was used as the basis for the development of a battlefield version, the Mark I, which entered combat in 1916. This machine exhibited the classic shape of the World War I tank—the rhomboid—chosen to aid the vehicle in crossing wide trenches without becoming wedged in. Various improvements of the Mark I were built as the war progressed. These early tanks were armed with machine guns or small caliber cannons, but they were slow and mechanically unreliable.

British tanks first fought at the Battle of the Somme and Ancre rivers in September, 1916. A total of forty-nine tanks began the assault from their assembly point. Only thirty-two tanks arrived at the front lines and just nine vehicles were able to cross No Man's Land. Because of numerous mechanical breakdowns and the lack of effective battle tactics, this initial engagement did not prove to be an important element of the battle. The armored tank concept was eventually proven effective as a decisive weapon at the Battle of Cambrai, in November of 1917. With a large assembly of 400 tanks advancing en masse, the British swept to a crushing victory, capturing over 30,000 German soldiers. From that point on, the tank became a necessary element in future land battles. Several different nations fielded armored tanks during World War I including France, Italy, and Germany.

Other types of armored fighting vehicles were also used during the First World War. Wheeled vehicles known as armored cars were deployed for scouting and infantry support. Although they could not cross some of the most devastated battlefields alongside the track-driven tanks, they were faster, more maneuverable, and had greater range over open country or roadways. Post-World War I developments in fighting vehicles included armored personnel carriers, used for troop transport and protection in the battlefield area.

The development of battle tanks during the inter-war years, 1918–1939, moved at a slow pace in Britain, France, and the United States. In Germany, however, immense resources of money, manpower, and technical expertise were devoted to the design and production of advanced tanks, aircraft, and other military equipment. When World War II began in 1939, the German invasion of Poland was spearheaded by thousands of fast and well-armed *Panzer Kampfwagens* (armored fighting vehicles). These tanks were deployed with well-conceived battle tactics that quickly overcame the Polish defenders.

The same method of tank warfare—*blitzkrieg* or lightning war—was used in 1940 to defeat the French army. When Great Britain entered the war in 1940, they deployed a number of light and medium tanks which they called cruiser tanks and infantry tanks. They were used in

North Africa during the first large-scale tank battles of the war against the German Afrika Korps Panzer tanks. Under the command of the brilliant German tank warfare strategist, Field Marshall Erwin Rommel, the Afrika Korps scored many victories in the desert campaign. They were finally defeated and broken at the second Battle of El-Alamein by British and American forces. The greatest tank battles in the history of land warfare occurred near the Russian city of Kursk, in 1943. The Germans advanced toward that city with 2,380 tanks and were opposed by the Russian defenders with 3,300 tanks. In a single battle near Kursk in July, 1943, 700 German tanks fought 850 Russian tanks to an inconclusive standoff.

With the American entry into the war in 1941, the immense economic and industrial might of the United States became the "arsenal of democracy" for the Allied forces. American tanks, aircraft, ships, trucks, and artillery were rugged, reliable, easy to repair, and they were produced in immense quantities far in excess of the Axis powers' capabilities. The principal tank deployed by the American forces, the M4 Sherman, was built with a total production of an amazing 49,230 vehicles.

In the post-war years, tank development was spurred on by the cold war between the free world democracies, led by the United States, and the Communist dictatorships, dominated by the Soviet Union (Russia). Each side competed with the other in an arms race to maintain a military advantage. It was during this era that a deadly new type of tank gun ammunition was devised. First used in the British Centurion tank, this potent shell was called an armor-piercing discarding sabot (APDS) round. It consisted of a strengthened steel spike guided by fins, and enclosed in a light metal jacket that was the diameter of the gun bore (inside gun barrel diameter). The jacket was discarded after the round left the gun, sending the finned spike toward the enemy tank at extremely high velocity. This type of ammunition is able to penetrate many inches of steel armor, making it a deadly tank killer.

To counter the APDS and other new types of high explosive tank munitions, modern tanks have been built with advanced armor protection. Exotic composites of ceramic, steel, and plastic laminates that are able to resist great heat and impact now cover the critical areas of tanks. Top-secret layers of Stillbrew and Chobham armor cover British tanks, making them almost impervious to enemy gunfire. The American M1A1 Abrams main battle tank (MBT) has been fitted with additional armor made from depleted uranium, a substance two and one-half times more dense than steel. Another type of protection called explosive reactive armor can be added over the tanks' regular armor. This system incorporates steel boxes with explosives sandwiched between the steel plates. They are attached to the turret and hull of the tank. When the boxes are struck by an enemy tank round, they explode outward, directing the blast energy away from the tank.

The current generation of main battle tanks are fearsome and formidable armored vehicles. They have become the dominant force in modern land warfare. The twenty-first century will undoubtedly see tanks develop into even more advanced and powerful fighting machines.

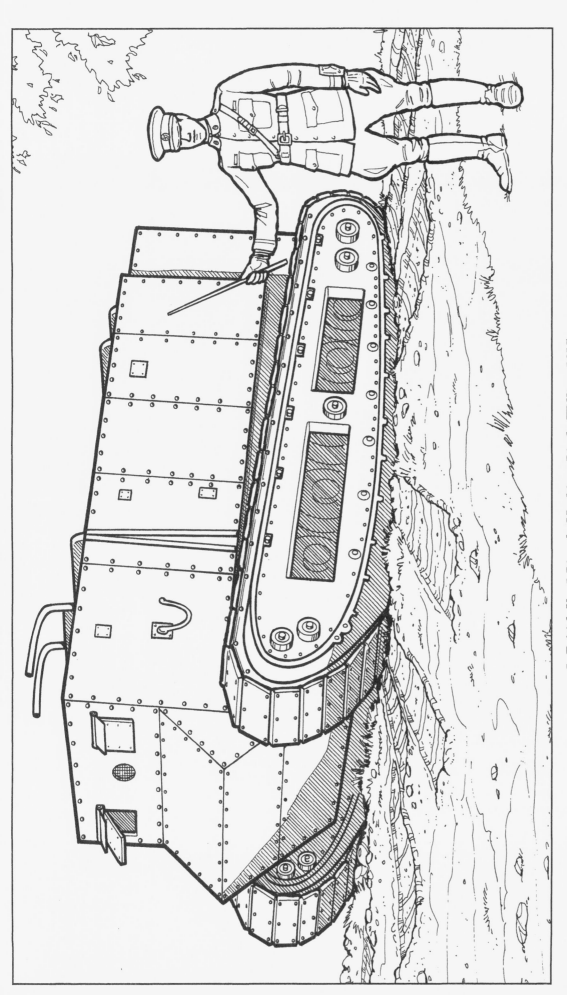

1. British No. 1 Lincoln Machine, *Little Willie*—1915

In 1914, the British formed a committee to secretly develop an armored, track-driven vehicle called a landship. This group included Army Colonel E. D. Swinton, naval officer Walter Wilson, and Sir William Tritton. They believed that the American Holt agricultural tractor might make a suitable foundation for their landship. The Holt tractor had continuous loop tracks on each side of the vehicle that could propel it through soft, muddy terrain which would normally bog down a wheeled vehicle. The landship committee tested the Holt tractor and two other tracked vehicles. The tests proved successful enough to warrant construction of their own design in 1915, the No. 1 Lincoln Machine. It consisted of a large armor-plated box with two 12-foot long tracks on each side. This first demonstration vehicle was nicknamed *Little Willie*. The testing of *Little Willie* was done under conditions of top secret security. To mislead possible enemy spies, the vehicle was referred to as a mobile, towed water tank, to be used for troops at the front. The name "tank" soon became the common term for successive armored fighting vehicles. *Little Willie* was painted a dark green color.

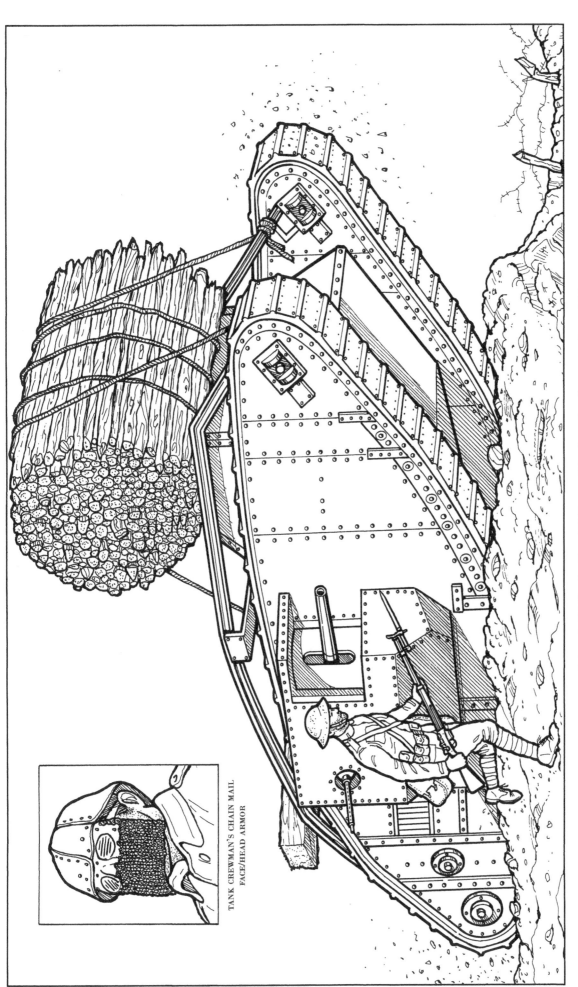

TANK CREWMAN'S CHAIN MAIL
FACE/HEAD ARMOR

2. British Mark IV Tank, *Big Willie* or *Mother* (male version)—1916

The development of a battlefield version of *Little Willie* was begun in 1916. These first battle tanks progressed through several models from the Mark I to the Mark V. They were variously nicknamed both *Big Willie* and *Mother*. Shown above is a 1917 Mark IV version. It was 26 feet long, 13 feet wide, and 8 feet high. To propel its 65,120-lb. weight, the Mark IV had a 150-hp gasoline engine. It could attain a turtle-like top speed of just 4 mph. It was covered with steel-plate armor with an average thickness of 0.39 inches. Since the armor plating was riveted in place, enemy gunfire often popped these metal studs, sending them flying around the interior of

and face-guards made of chain mail, much like that of a medieval knight. The Mark IV was produced in two versions, designated as male and female. The male version shown above was armed with two 6-pounder guns and four .303-caliber machine guns. The female version was armed with four .303-caliber machine guns. The Mark IV had a range of 15 miles and was operated by a crew of 8 men. Shown on top of the tank is a bundle of sticks and planks that were dropped into the open trenches to create a makeshift bridge to span the trench. These early British battle tanks were painted in solid dark green, and in various camouflage designs showing irregular

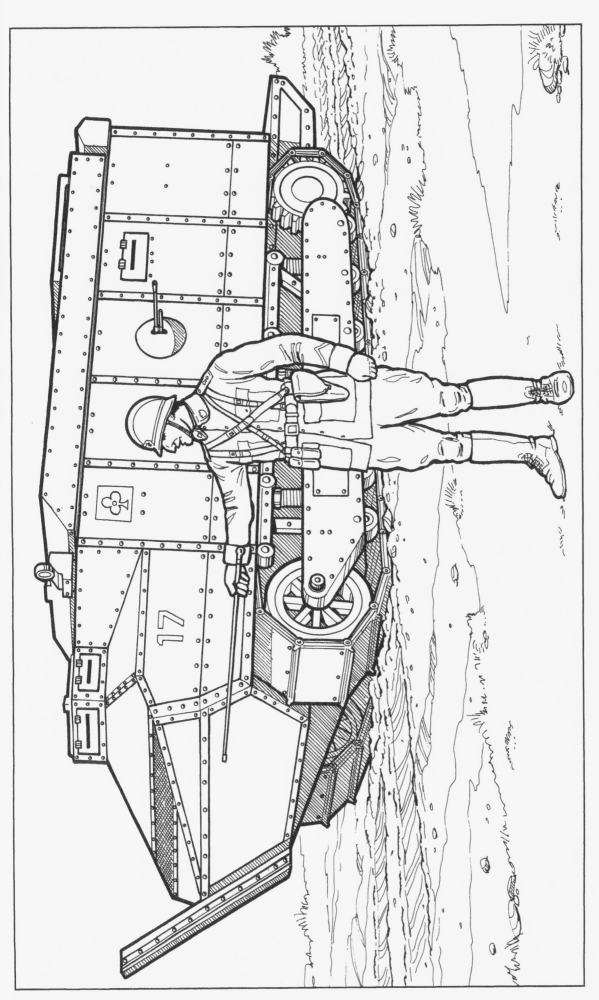

3. French *Char d'Assaut* Schneider Tank—1916

The first French tank developed for use in World War I is pictured above. It is the *Char d'Assaut* (attack car) Schneider tank, introduced for battlefield use in 1916. The Schneider tank was 20 feet long, 6½ feet wide, and 7½ feet high. It weighed 32,560 lb. and was driven by a 4-cylinder, 60-hp gasoline engine. The vehicle could reach a top speed of just 4 mph. It carried a 7-man crew to operate the tank and fire the guns. The Schneider was armed with a 75-mm main gun and 2 machine guns. It had a 48-mile range of action and an armor thickness of 0.45 inches. Shown in the illustration is a large steel beam attached to the front edge of the tank to batter and crush enemy barbed wire or other fortifications along the trench lines. The Schneider depicted above was painted in dark olive green camouflage.

4. British Rolls Royce Armored Scout Car—1916

Depicted above is a British armored scout car widely used during World War I. It was built with a Rolls Royce chassis and engine, and fitted with armor averaging 0.35 inches in thickness. The vehicle was 17 feet long, 6 feet wide, and 8 feet high at the top of its revolving armored turret. Within the turret was a Vickers .303-caliber machine gun. Its 50-hp gasoline engine could propel the 7,480-lb. car to a speed of 60 mph with a 150-mile range of action. The armored car normally carried a crew of 4 for scouting and reconnaissance missions. The vehicle was painted either medium gray or desert tan.

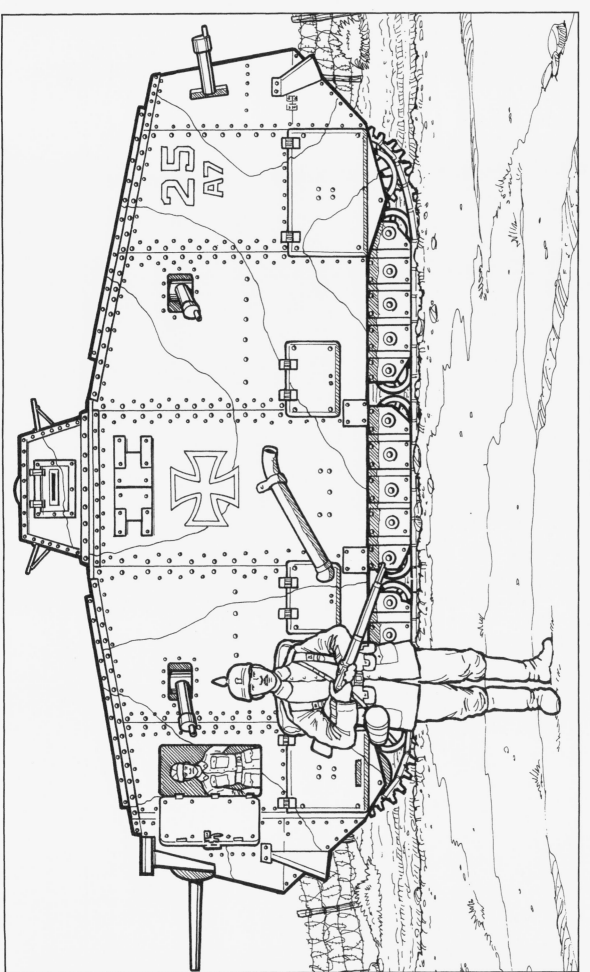

5. German A7V *SturmPanzerwagen* Tank—1917

The only German tank to engage in combat operations during the First World War was the enormous A7V *SturmPanzerwagen*. The A7V stood 10½ feet high, was 26 feet long, and had a width of 10 feet. A crew of 18 men was required to operate this massive tank! It was armed with a main gun of 57-mm caliber and 6 other machine guns. The A7V was equipped with two 100-hp gasoline engines to move its 73,000 lb. of weight. It could reach a speed of only 5 mph, and was extremely cumbersome and difficult to maneuver. Only 20 *SturmPanzerwagens* were built during the war, and their great size and clumsiness made them a very ineffective fighting machine. The A7V shown above was painted in a mottled camouflage design of dark olive green and earth brown splotches.

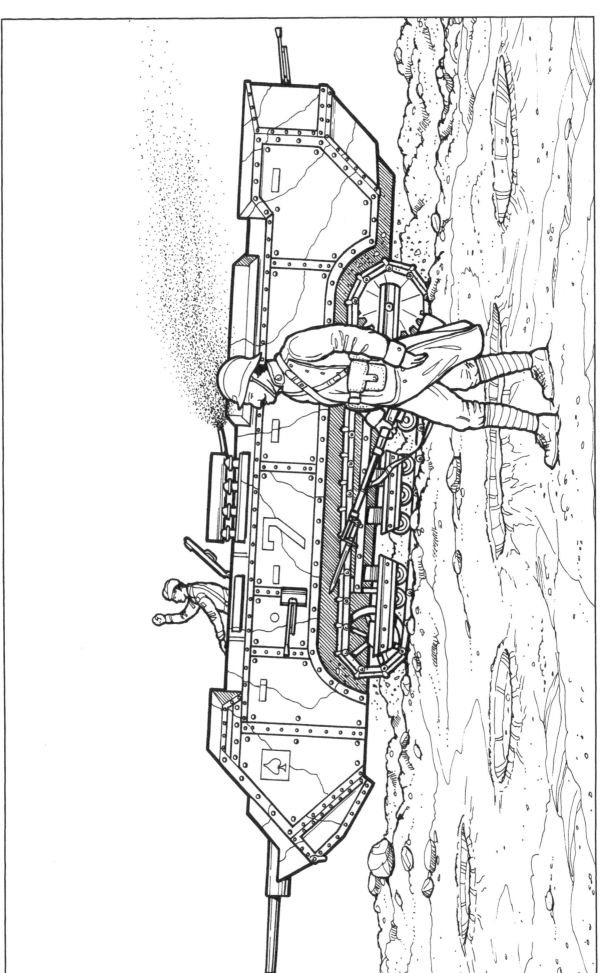

6. French *Char d'Assaut* St. Chamond Tank—1916

Another large French tank fielded during the war was the *Char d'Assaut* St. Chamond, pictured above. It had a weight of 51,800 lb., a speed of 5.3 mph, and a 36-mile range. The vehicle was 28½ feet long, 8½ feet wide, and 7½ feet high. Its armor plating was 0.67 inches thick. The St. Chamond was armed with a 75-mm main gun, and up to 4 additional 7.5-mm machine guns. It was powered by a 90-hp 4-cylinder gasoline engine, and carried a crew of 9 men. The color scheme for the St. Chamond above is a tan, brown, and green mottled camouflage.

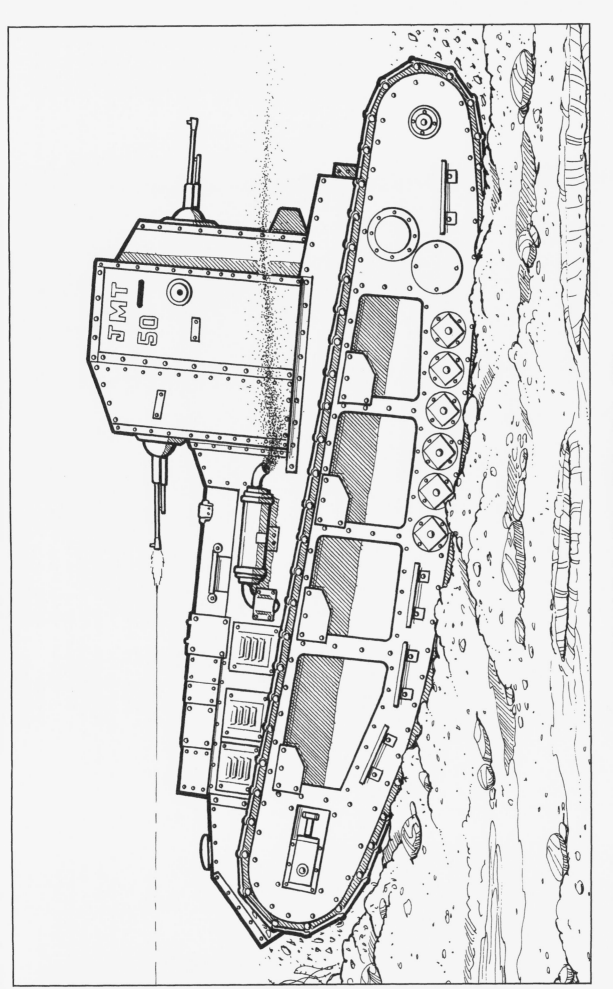

7. British Mark A Whippet Medium Tank—1917

The tank depicted above is the British Mark A Whippet, introduced in 1917. It was designed to break through enemy lines and disrupt German rear areas past the trench lines. It was driven by two 45-hp, 4-cylinder gasoline engines mounted in the front. These gave the Whippet the comparatively fast speed of 8.3 mph. It had 2 or 3 Hotchkiss .303-caliber machine guns mounted in a fixed, non-revolving turret at the rear. Armor plating averaging 0.55 inches thick protected the 3-man crew. The vehicle was 20 feet long, 8½ feet wide, and 9 feet high. It weighed 31,460 lb. and had a range of 160 miles. The Whippet was painted in dark olive green camouflage.

8. French Renault FT 17 Light Tank—1917

The French army developed a very capable light tank in 1917. Pictured above is the Renault FT 17, the first tank to enter combat operations with a turret able to revolve in a complete 360° circle. This gave the vehicle a very flexible and effective means of firing its guns during battle. It was relatively small by tank standards, with a crew of just 2 men. The FT 17 was 13 feet long, 5½ feet wide, and reached a height of 7 feet. With its 35-hp 4-cylinder gasoline engine, the vehicle could traverse open country at 5 mph. To protect the crew, the FT 17 had armor plating that was 0.63 inches thick. The little tank was armed with either a 37-mm cannon or an 8-mm machine gun. The version illustrated is equipped with the 37-mm cannon in its rotating turret. The vehicle weighed 14,520 lb, and had a range of 22 miles. Over 3,000 FT 17's were produced during the war, and proved to be a very capable tactical weapon for trench warfare. At the Battle of Soissons in July of 1918, 480 FT 17's were used to contribute to the French victory. The FT 17 was painted in medium gray, dark olive green, or in a tan, brown, and green mottled camouflage design.

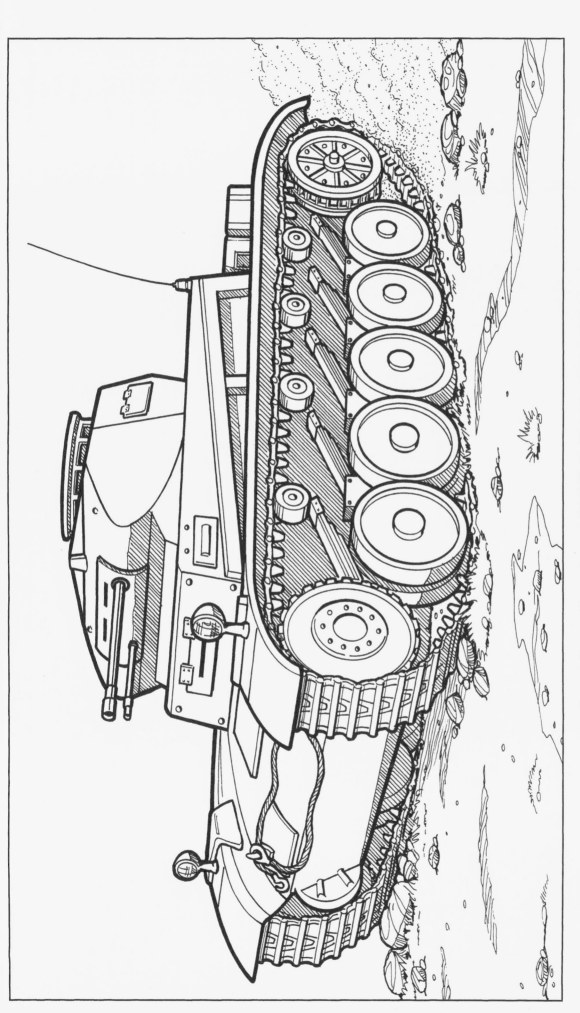

9. German Panzer *Kampfwagen* II (PzKpfw II) Light Tank—1935

The first Panzers were light tanks. They were quite fast by the standards of the day, but carried small caliber guns and thin armor. As the war continued during the early 1940s, successive versions of the Panzers became larger and much more heavily armed and armored. The Panzer I was fitted with two 7.92-mm machine guns in its revolving turret. The Panzer II, pictured above, was armed with a 20-mm cannon and a 7.92-mm machine gun, making it a more deadly fighting machine. Its main gun could penetrate 1-inch thick enemy tank armor at a distance of 500 yards. The Panzer II was powered by a 140-hp Maybach 6-cylinder gasoline engine which gave the vehicle a top speed of 34 mph. It was protected by 1.38-inch thick armor on the turret and hull. The 22,046-lb. vehicle was 15 feet long, 7½ feet wide, and 7½ feet high. With its crew of 3 men, the Panzer II had a combat range of 125 miles. In the 1941 German invasion of Russia, over 1,000 Panzer tanks were fielded in the first attack. The early Panzer tanks were painted in a medium dull-gray finish.

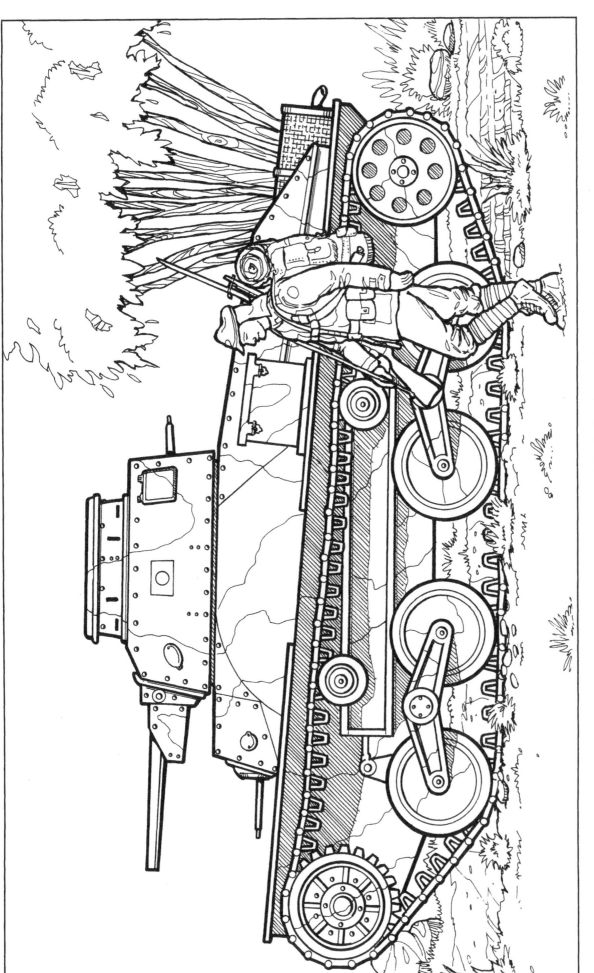

10. Japanese Type 95 KE-GO Light Tank—1935

The Japanese imperial forces did not rely heavily on tank warfare in their invasions of China and other Asian countries during World War II. Their most widely used fighting tank was the Type 95 KE-GO light tank, developed in 1935 and shown above. This vehicle was lightly armored and fitted with a small caliber main gun. When faced with American medium tanks in the Pacific islands war, the Type 95 was easily destroyed. The KE-GO was armed with a 37-mm cannon and two 7.7-mm machine guns. It carried armor plating that ranged from 0.25 to 0.6 inches in thickness. The vehicle was 14½ feet long, 6½ feet wide, and was 7 feet high at the top of its turret. It was powered by a Mitsubishi 6-cylinder air-cooled diesel engine of 128 hp. The 16,280-lb. vehicle could reach a speed of 20 mph over open country. It carried a crew of 4 men. The one depicted above was painted in a jungle camouflage of mottled tan, green, and dark gray splotches.

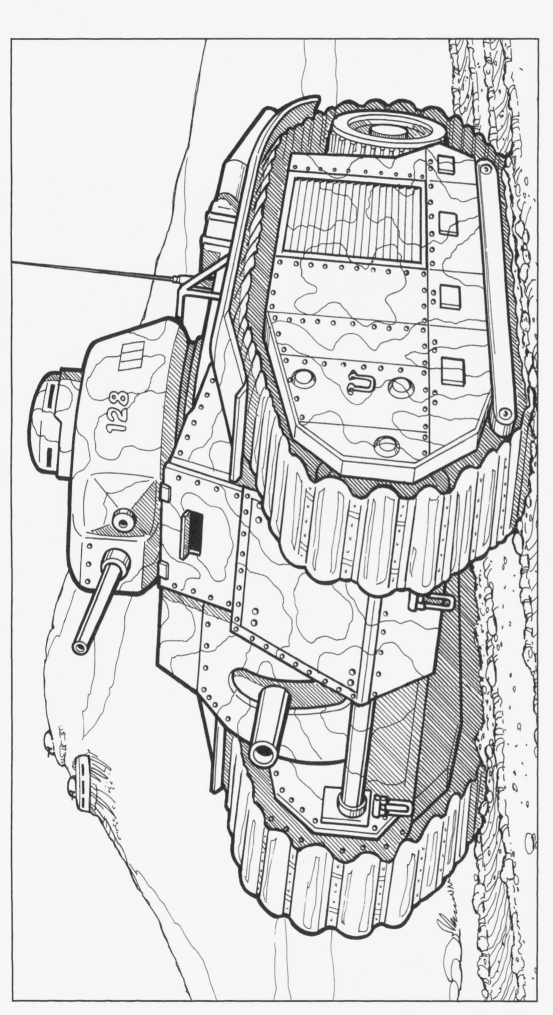

11. French *Char* B1 Heavy Tank—1937

The *Char* B1 heavy tank depicted above was introduced in 1937, and used by the French in their defense against the German invasion of 1940. It was a formidable and powerful fighting vehicle, but was overcome by superior German tank warfare tactics. It was well armored with protection ranging from 0.6 to 2.5 inches of steel plating, and was equipped with self-sealing fuel tanks to reduce the chances of fire and explosion from a hit by an enemy tank. The B1 was heavily armed with a 75-mm main gun mounted in the front of the hull. It could traverse up and down but not side to side. The entire tank would have to move to change its lateral firing direction. In the B1's revolving turret, another cannon of 45-mm caliber was mounted. The vehicle was also equipped with one or two 7.5-mm machine guns. The B1 was 20½ feet long, 8 feet wide, and 9 feet high. It weighed a hefty 69,300 lb. With its Renault 6-cylinder 307-hp gasoline engine, the tank could reach 17.5 mph and had an action range of 112 miles. A crew of four tankers operated this powerful fighting machine. When the French army was defeated by the Germans in 1940, captured B1 tanks were used to train German tankers and also as stationary artillery emplacements. The B1 was painted in a multicolor camouflage scheme of dark brown, dark green, and dark gray. It is depicted above with Maginot line hilltop forts in the background.

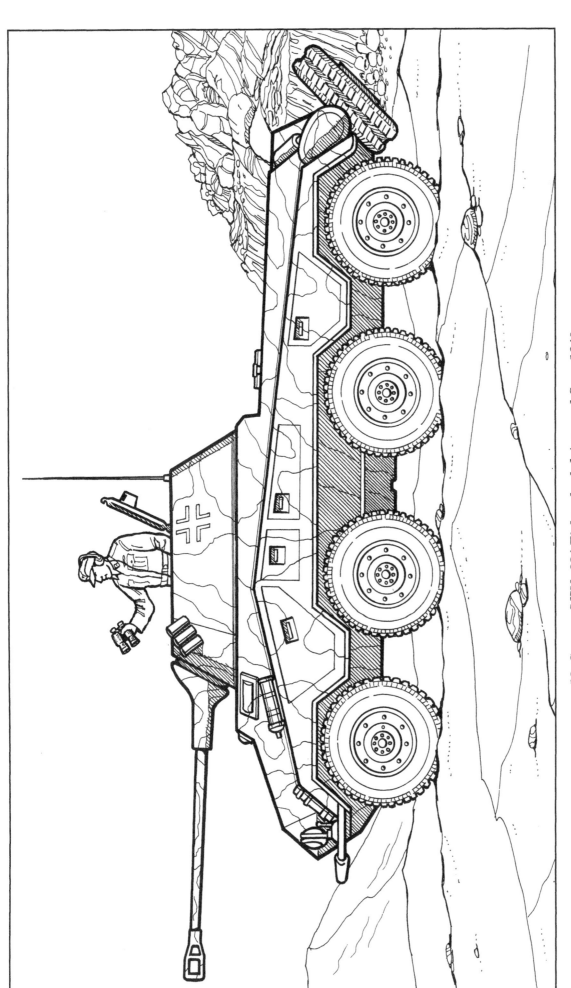

12. German SdKfz 234 Eight-wheeled Armored Car—1940

The German army fielded a number of well-armored and powerfully-gunned scout cars during World War II. Pictured above is a vehicle specifically designed for use by the German Afrika Korps in their desert war in North Africa. It was a large vehicle with a weight of 25,828 lb. and armor protection ranging from 0.19 to 0.59 inches in thickness. The SdKfz 234 was fitted with many different gun types, ranging from machine guns to anti-aircraft guns to cannons. The version shown mounts a 50-mm cannon and a coaxial 7.92-mm machine gun in its revolving turret. The term coaxial refers to a gun mounted alongside another gun on the same axis (pointing in the same direction). This is a common practice among tanks and armored vehicles. The SdKfz 234 carried a crew of 4 and was powered by a Tatra diesel engine developing 210 hp. It had a road speed of 53 mph and a combat range of 625 miles. This particular armored car was produced throughout the war and used in all combat theatres. It is generally considered to be the best armored reconnaisance vehicle of World War II. The vehicle was painted in either solid desert tan, or a mottled camouflage design of irregular tan and brown swirls, stripes, or splotches.

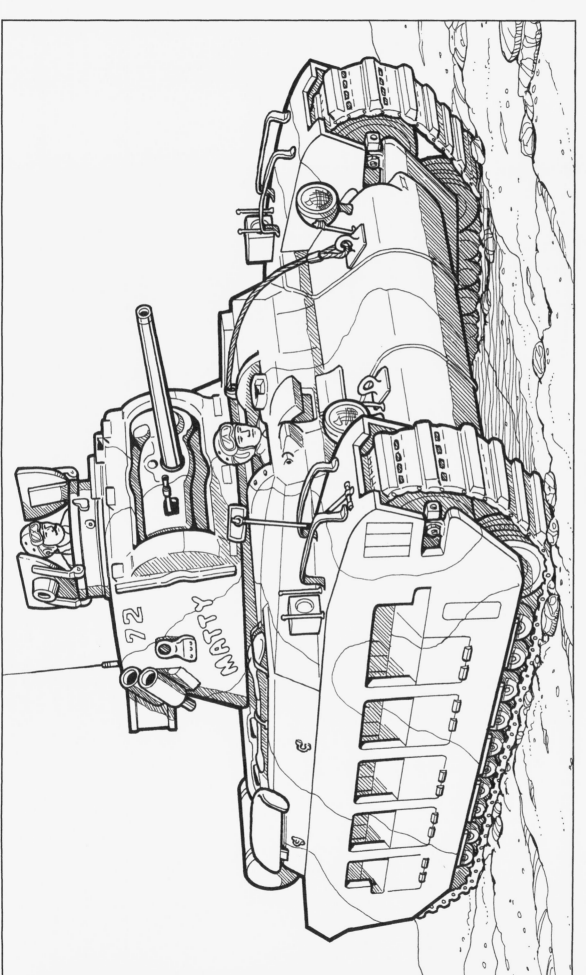

13. British A12 Matilda Infantry Tank—1940

One of the most widely used British tanks of the early war years was the A12 Matilda. It was mainly used to support and provide firepower for advancing infantry troops. The Matilda was built with armor plating up to 3.1 inches thick, fairly heavy protection for that period. It was undergunned, however, with its main gun only a 2-pounder (40-mm) cannon. With its strong armored hull and turret, the Matilda could withstand a hit from a Panzer II 20-mm main gun or a 37-mm anti-tank gun. The vehicle was 19 feet long, 8½ feet wide, and 8½ feet high. It weighed 50,237 lb. and was driven by two 87-hp diesel engines giving it a top speed of 15 mph. The Matilda was manned by a crew of 4 and had a cruising range of 160 miles. The Matildas used in the North African campaign were usually painted in a desert tan camouflage paint scheme.

14. German Panzer *Kampfwagen* III (PzKpfw III) Medium Tank—1940

With the introduction of this version of their famous Panzer tank, the Panzer III, the German army had a fighting vehicle that was well-armored, fast, and equipped with a powerful main gun. Initially entering combat in 1940 with a 50-mm turret-mounted gun, the Panzer III was soon upgunned to a high velocity 75-mm cannon. It was additionally armed with a 7.92-mm machine gun. With an average armor thickness of 1.118 inches, the Panzer III weighed in at 49,060 lb. It was powered by a Maybach 12-cylinder, 300-hp gasoline engine, giving the vehicle a cross-country speed of 25 mph and an action range of 110 miles. With a crew of 5 tankers, the Panzer III was 21 feet long, 9½ feet wide, and 8 feet high. Panzer III tanks were painted either dull gray or in a camouflage design of irregular splotches of tan, brown, and green.

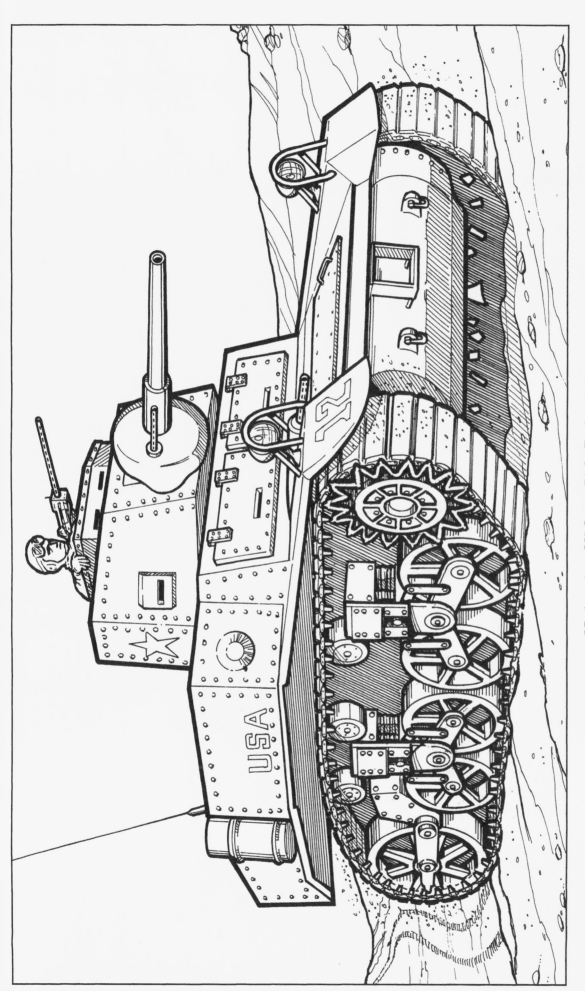

15. American M3 Stuart Light Tank—1940

The tank initially used by the United States in World War II was the M3 Stuart light tank. It was also exported to the British army in great numbers before the U.S. entered the war. Initially introduced in 1941 with its armor riveted to the hull and turret, the Stuart was soon modified with a more sturdy cast and welded armor. Its main turret guns were a 37-mm cannon and a .30-caliber machine gun mounted coaxially. The Stuart was also equipped with a .30-caliber machine gun mounted on top of the turret for anti-aircraft protection. With a weight of 28,440 lb. and a 6-cylinder radial engine developing 250 hp, the vehicle had a swift top speed of 36 mph. It was 14½ feet long, 7½ feet wide, and 7½ feet high. The Stuarts' crew of 4 men was protected by armor averaging 1.69 inches thick. Used by the Americans, British, and Russians, a total of 13,859 Stuart tanks were built from 1940 to 1943. The M3 Stuart tanks were normally painted either desert tan for use in Africa, or olive drab green for the European theater.

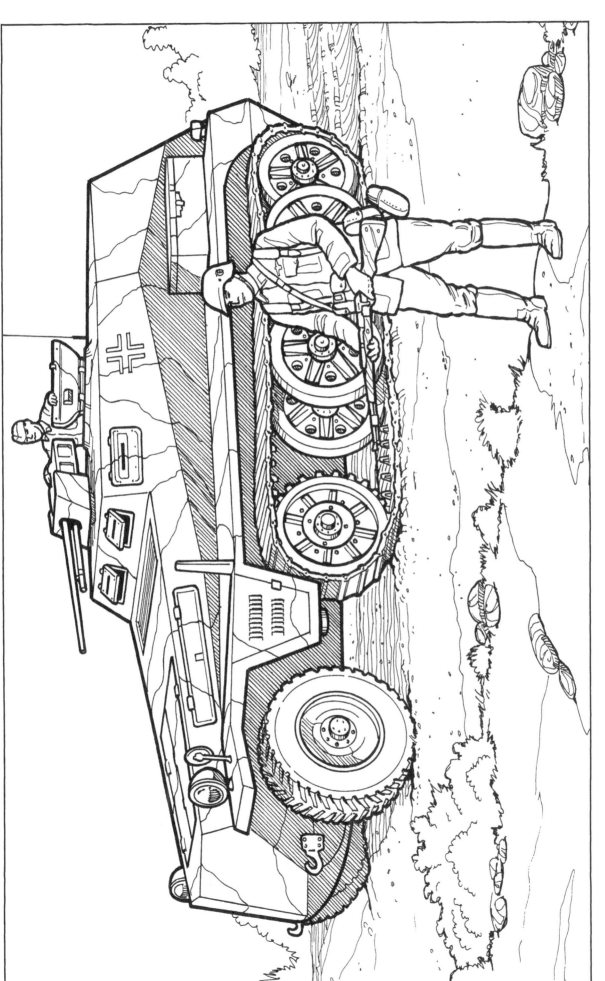

16. German SdKfz 250 Half-track Armored Personnel Carrier—1939

A large armored vehicle used by the German army during the war was the SdKfz 250 half-track armored personnel carrier. As illustrated above, the vehicle featured wheels at the front and tank-type tracks at the rear. It could carry a combination of 6 crewmen and infantry soldiers, and be equipped with a variety of weapons including machine guns, anti-aircraft guns, or a 37-mm anti-tank gun as depicted above. It was 19 feet long, 6½ feet wide, and 6 feet high. With its 100-hp gasoline engine, the SdKfz 250 could reach 32 mph. It had armor plating averaging 0.5 inches thick and weighed 17,182 lb. German armored cars used in Europe were painted in a number of different camouflage designs using tan, brown, green, and black.

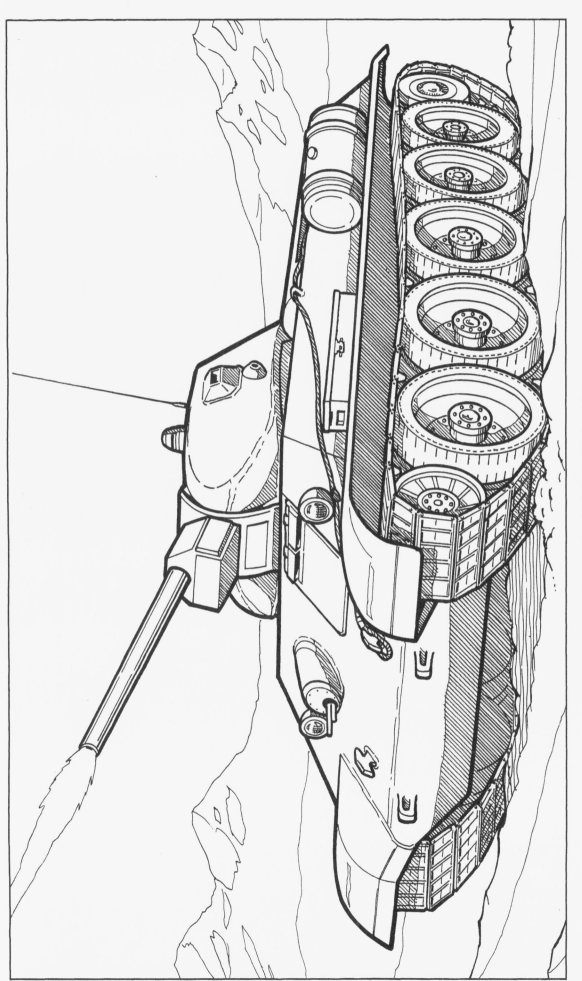

17. Russian T-34 Medium Tank—1940

One of the most successful tank designs to come out of World War II was the formidable T-34 medium tank fielded by the Russian army. Its powerful main gun and innovative sloped armored turret made it a match for any German tank. In addition to the T-34's armor and gun, it was also very fast and maneuverable, with a top speed of 34 mph. Powering this 57,200-lb. fighting machine was a V-12 diesel engine generating 500 hp. Initially equipped with a high-velocity 76-mm main gun, the T-34 was upgunned with an 85-mm cannon in 1944. Both weapons could penetrate the armor of a German Panzer III or IV tank at a distance of 500 yards. The armor on the T-34 was up to 2.36 inches thick on its sloped turret. The T-34 was 19½ feet long, 9½ feet wide, and 8 feet high. It was operated by 4 crewmen. During the Soviet Union's struggle against the German invasion (1941–1944), over 40,000 T-34 tanks were produced. Russian tanks were painted either dark olive green, medium gray, or white, depending on the area of operations.

18. American M3 Half-track Infantry Vehicle—1941

The American M3 half-track infantry vehicle was produced in huge numbers and served with the U.S. army and its allies during and after the Second World War. Forty-one thousand of these workhorse vehicles were built during the wartime era. The M3 was normally armed with one .50-caliber machine gun and one .30-caliber machine gun, but was modified with many different types of equipment for a variety of uses. Its usual manpower complement was a crew of 3 plus 10 fully-equipped troops. The vehicle was 20½ feet long, 7 feet wide, and 7½ feet high. With a weight of 20,458 lb., the M3 could attain a speed of 40 mph powered by its 147-hp six-cylinder gasoline engine. It had a cruising range of 175 miles and featured .031-inch thick armor to protect the crew and infantrymen. The M3 was normally painted olive drab green.

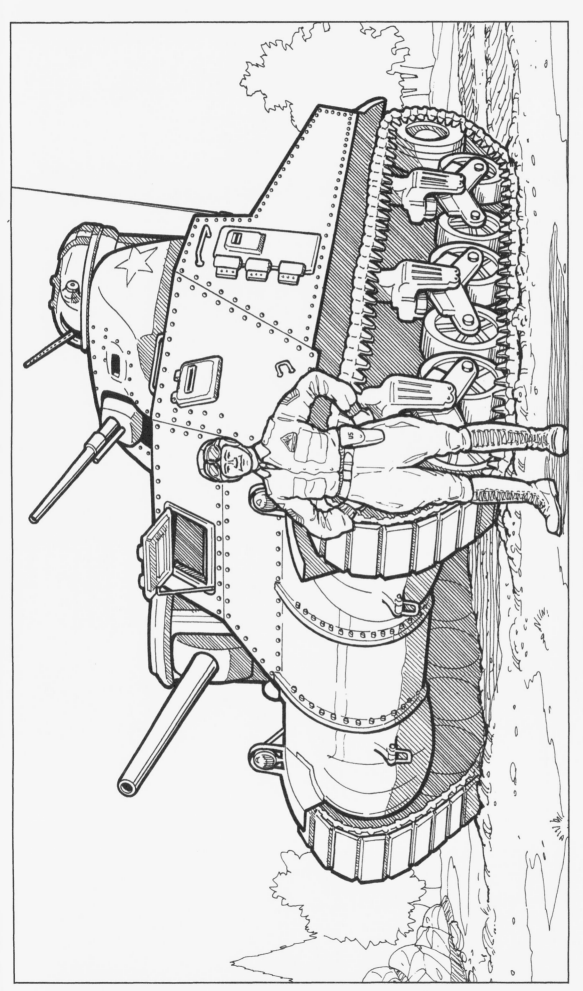

19. American M3 Grant/Lee Medium Tank—1941

The powerful and effective American M3 medium tank was introduced in 1941. It first saw action with the British in their North Africa campaign against Rommel's Afrika Korps in May of 1942. The M3 was called the General Grant in British service and the General Lee in the American armored forces. It was fitted with a 75-mm cannon located in the front of the hull. This main gun was able to move up and down, and to a more limited degree, from side to side. Inside the M3's revolving top turret was mounted a 30-mm cannon, with a .30-caliber machine gun located in a smaller rotating cupola atop the turret. (A cupola is a smaller raised blister at the top of a tank used by the vehicle's commander.) The vehicle had armor protection up to 1.5 inches thick. To power the 59,928-lb. vehicle, a 9-cylinder radial air-cooled aircraft engine producing 340 hp was normally installed. The M3 had a fighting range of 120 miles. It was quite a massive tank with a length of 18½ feet, a width of 8½ feet, and a height of 10 feet. The M3's crew complement was 6 tankers. The vehicles were painted either desert tan for North Africa or olive drab green for Europe.

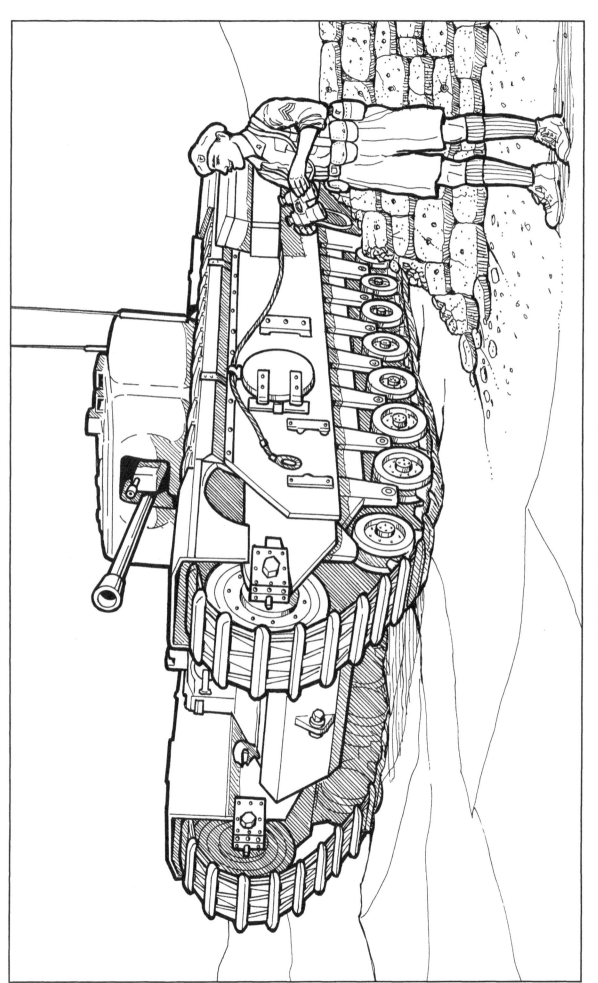

20. British A22 Churchill Infantry Tank—1942

A mainstay of British armored forces during World War II was the robust A22 Churchill infantry tank pictured above. It was heavily armored and carried a more powerful gun than the Matilda, described earlier. Its turret-mounted cannon fired a 6-pounder shell that was effective against all but the largest German Panzer tanks. Alongside the main gun the Churchill also featured a 7.62-mm machine gun. The turret was protected by up to 4 inches of steel armor. The Churchill had a weight of 89,412 lb. and a length of 24½ feet. Because of its considerable size and weight, the Churchill was quite slow, only able to reach 13 mph with its 12-cylinder gasoline engine of 304 hp. The tank carried a crew of 5 men and had an action range of 90 miles. Shown above is a tank from the North African desert campaign that would have been painted in a desert tan color.

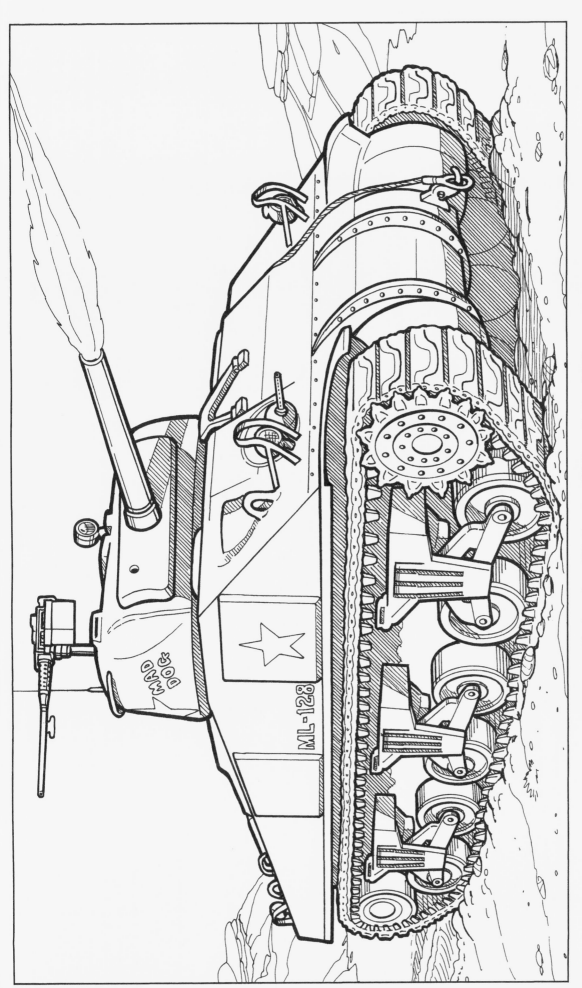

21. American M4 Sherman Medium Tank—1942

A successor to the M3 Grant/Lee medium tank, the M4 Sherman became the principle tank of American armored forces from 1942 until the end of the war in 1945. Like the Grant/Lee, the Sherman was very rugged, reliable, and easy to maintain and repair. It initially mounted a 75-mm cannon on its rounded, armored turret. It also carried a .30-caliber machine gun located in the front of the hull and a .50-caliber machine gun on top of the turret. Although the Sherman was a heavy vehicle, it had a good road speed of 29 mph. It weighed 69,000 lb. and was powered by two General Motors diesel engines generating 500 hp. The M4 was 19½ feet long, 8½ feet wide, and 9 feet high. It was manned by a crew of 5 and had a combat range of 100 miles. Later versions of the Sherman were upgunned with a 76-mm high-velocity cannon that could punch through 4 inches of German armor at a distance of 500 yards. A number of special versions were even equipped with a very powerful 90-mm cannon and used as tank destroyers.

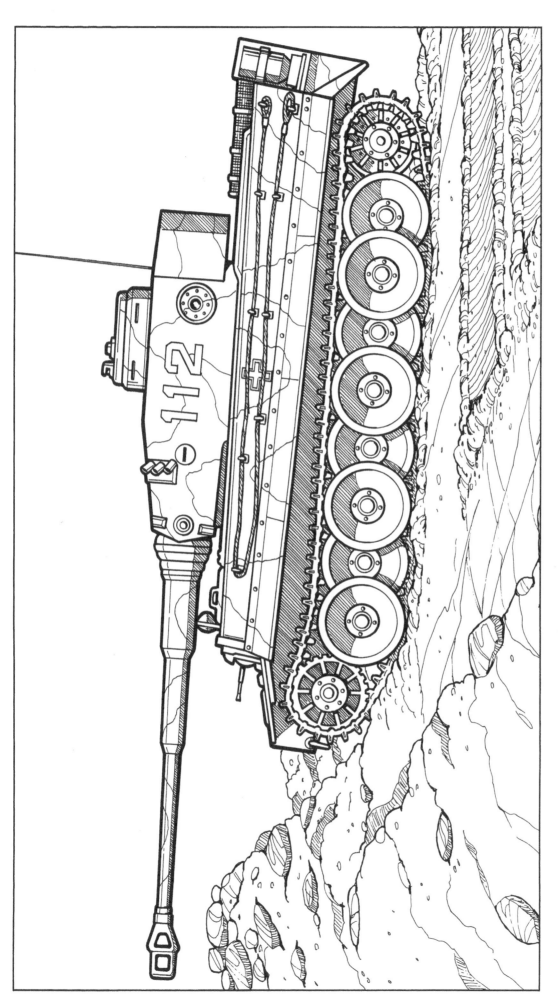

22. German Panzer VI Tiger I Heavy Tank—1942

When an Allied tank crew encountered the dreaded German Tiger tank, they knew it would be a tough battle. Its powerful 88-mm main gun could shatter the armor of any British, American, or Russian tank. Combined with 4-inch thick armor protection, the Tiger was a very dangerous fighting vehicle to tangle with. Most Allied tanks chose to attack a Tiger in numbers, hoping to outflank the vehicle with their greater speed in order to get a shot at its less well-armored rear. It weighed an enormous 121,000 lb. and was powered by a Maybach 12-cylinder gasoline engine producing 700 hp. It was 27 feet long, 12 feet wide, and stood 9 feet high at the top of its sizeable turret. In addition to the Tiger's main gun, it was equipped with a 7.92-mm machine gun mounted coaxially, and a 7.92-mm machine located in the front of the hull. It was manned by a crew of 5 tankers and had a combat range of 62 miles. As powerful a tank as the Tiger was, it did have several weaknesses. It lacked speed and maneuverability, and its complex mechanical systems were subject to frequent breakdowns. Another chronic problem was caused by the overlapping road wheels that supported its tracks. They tended to jam with mud, stones, and ice, stopping the vehicle dead in its tracks. The Tiger depicted above was painted in tan-and-brown irregular camouflage splotches and stripes.

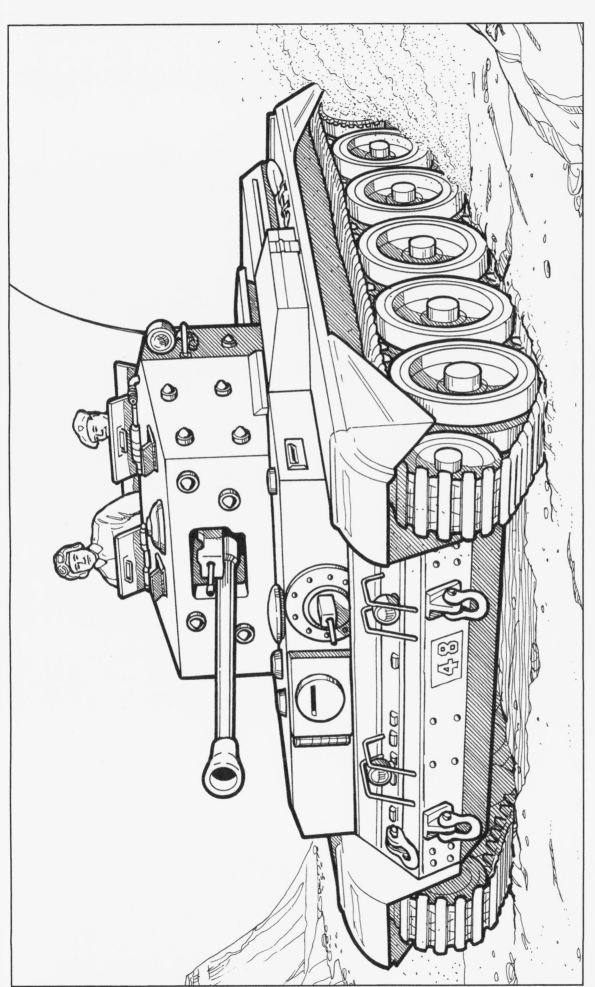

23. British A27 Cromwell Cruiser Tank—1943

The British introduced a fast and well-armored tank in 1943, the A27 Cromwell. It was initially equipped with a 6-pounder (57-mm) main gun, but that was soon found to be inadequate against the heavily armored German Tiger and Panther tanks. It was upgunned to a 75-mm cannon which gave it firepower on a par with the American Sherman tank. It was additionally armed with a coaxial 7.62-mm machine gun and a hull-mounted 7.62-mm machine gun. The Cromwell was powered by a Rolls Royce Meteor V-12 gasoline engine generating 570 hp. This gave the 61,472-lb. vehicle a top speed of 38 mph. The tank was 21 feet long, 10 feet wide, and 8 feet high. It was protected by armor up to 3 inches thick. Later versions of the Cromwell had an additional inch of armor plate bolted to the turret. The vehicle carried a crew of 5 men and had a range of 175 miles. Cromwells were painted either desert tan for Africa or dark green for Europe.

24. American M8 Greyhound Armored Scout Car—1943

The American M8 Greyhound armored car pictured above was widely deployed by Allied forces in both the European and Pacific theaters of war. It was a rugged and dependable vehicle with over 11,000 used in combat service. It was powered by a 6-cylinder gasoline engine putting out 110 hp and had a reconnaissance range of 350 miles. With a crew of 4 men, the M8 could reach a road speed of 60 mph. The vehicle was well-armed with a turret-mounted 37-mm cannon that could knock out light tanks and other armored vehicles. Mounted on top of the turret in a rotating ring was an additional .50-caliber machine gun. The Greyhound was protected by armor averaging .31 inches thick. It was 16½ feet long, 8½ feet wide, 7 feet high, and weighed 17,468 lb. M8 scout cars were most often painted standard U.S army olive drab green.

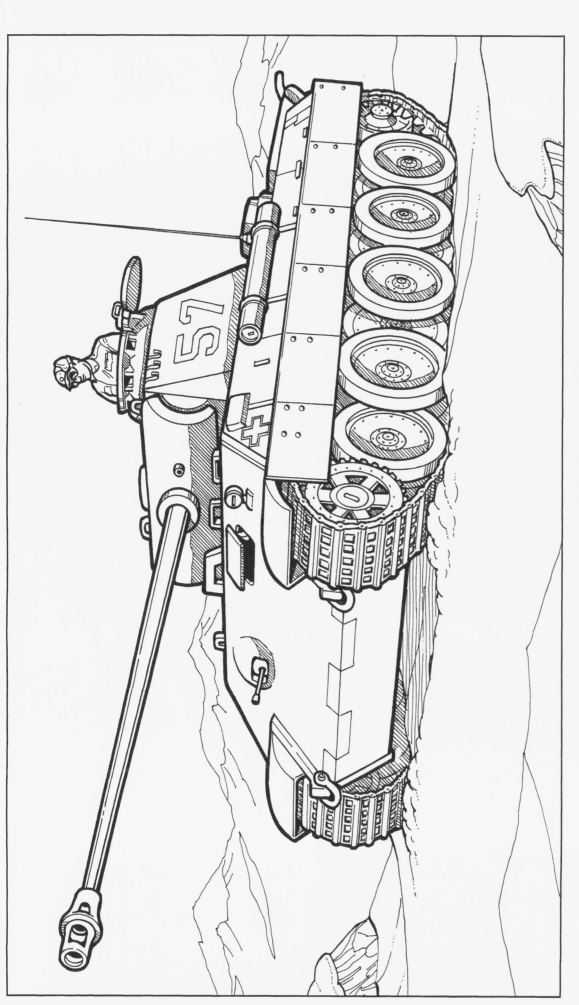

25. German Panzer V Panther Medium Tank—1943

Many military historians consider the Panzer V Panther to be the best fighting tank of World War II. It was developed specifically to combat the very effective Russian T-34 tank. It even incorporated the T-34's innovative sloped armor turret design. The Panther was armed with a long-barreled, high velocity 75-mm main gun. Shells from this powerful weapon could punch through 4 inches of sloped armor at a distance of 1,000 yards. It was also equipped with a coaxially-mounted 7.92-mm machine gun and a hull-mounted 7.92-mm machine gun. The tank was well protected with armor up to 4.3 inches thick on its sloped turret. The 100,100-lb. vehicle was powered by a Maybach 12-cylinder diesel engine developing 700 hp, giving it a road speed of 29 mph. The Panther was 29 feet long, 11 feet wide, and 10 feet high. With its crew of 5 men, the tank had a combat range of 110 miles. Panther tanks appeared in a variety of German camouflage designs incorporating mottled shapes and stripes of tan, brown, green, and dark gray

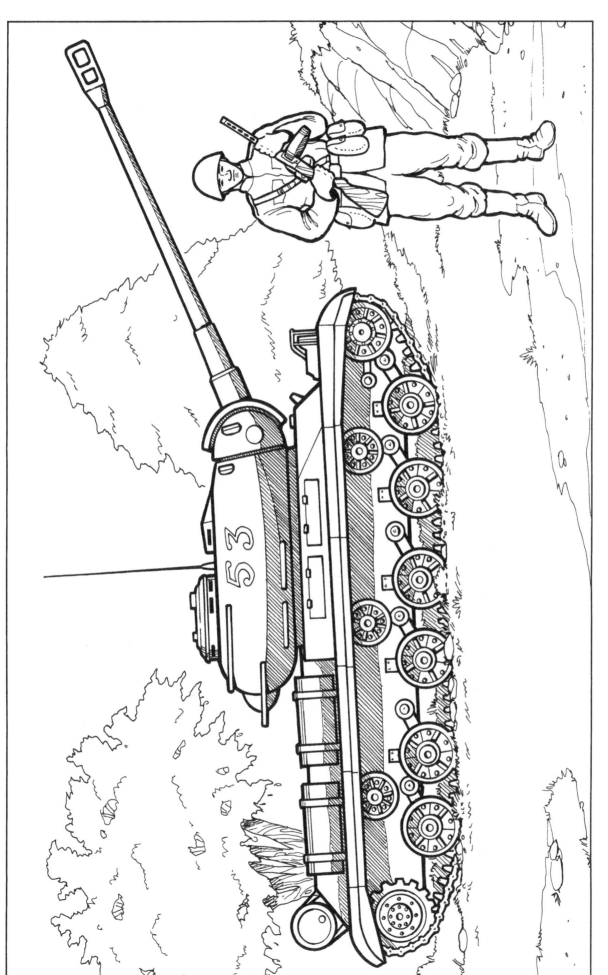

26. Russian IS-2 Joseph Stalin Heavy Tank—1943

The massive IS-2 Joseph Stalin was developed for the purpose of defeating the mighty German Tiger I and II tanks. It was equipped with the most powerful tank gun of the war, a massive 122-mm cannon capable of penetrating 6 inches of armor at 1,000 yards. Its secondary armament consisted of a 12.7-mm machine gun and a 7.62-mm machine gun. The IS-2 was also very well protected with armor that was up to 5.2 inches thick. The turret had a rounded inverted bowl shape that was very effective at deflecting enemy shells. The IS-2 was very large, with a length of 32 feet, width of 10 feet, and height of 8½ feet. The vehicle had a 600-hp V-12 diesel engine to propel its 101,200-lb. weight. It carried a crew of 4 tankers, had a top speed of 23 mph, and a range of 149 miles.

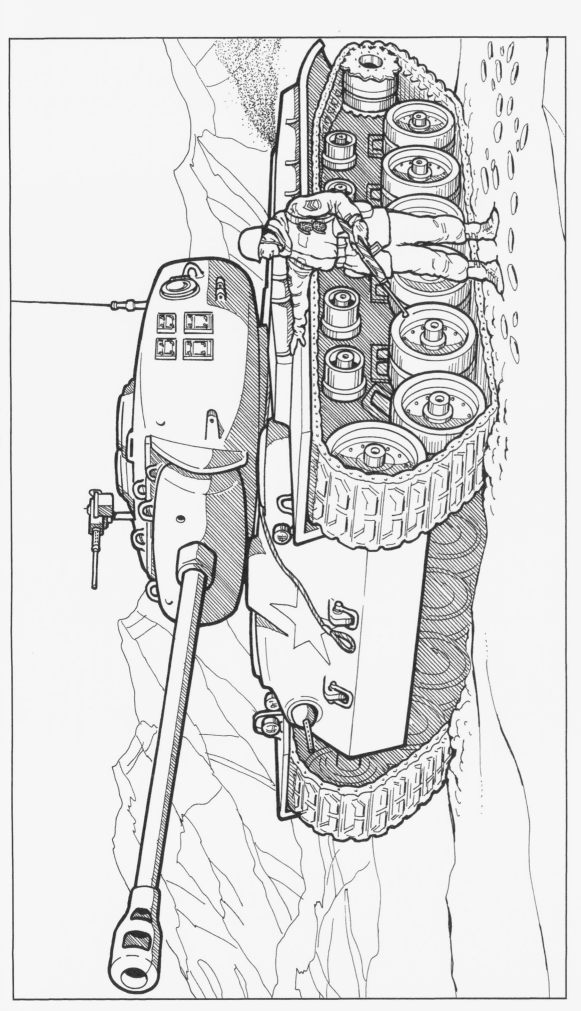

27. American M26 Pershing Heavy Tank—1945

The most powerful American tank of the Second World War arrived on the battle-fields just months before the end of the war. The M26 Pershing heavy tank saw limited action beginning in March 1945 when it faced German Tiger and Panther tanks at the Battle for Remagen Bridge. Its firepower and armor proved to be a match for the enemy tanks. The Pershing was fitted with a powerful 90-mm main gun, two .30-caliber machine guns, and a top-turret mounted .50-caliber machine gun. Its rounded turret was protected by up to 4 inches of armor. The big tank was 28 feet long, 11 feet wide, and 9 feet high. With a 500-hp V-8 gasoline engine, the M26 could reach a top speed of 30 mph. It weighed 93,355 lb. with a crew of 5 men, and had a fighting range of 100 miles. The M26 went on to serve very effectively during the Korean War (1950–1953), where it battled and defeated Russian T-34 tanks that had been upgunned with 85-mm cannons. American tanks of the 1950s and 60s were normally painted standard army olive drab green.

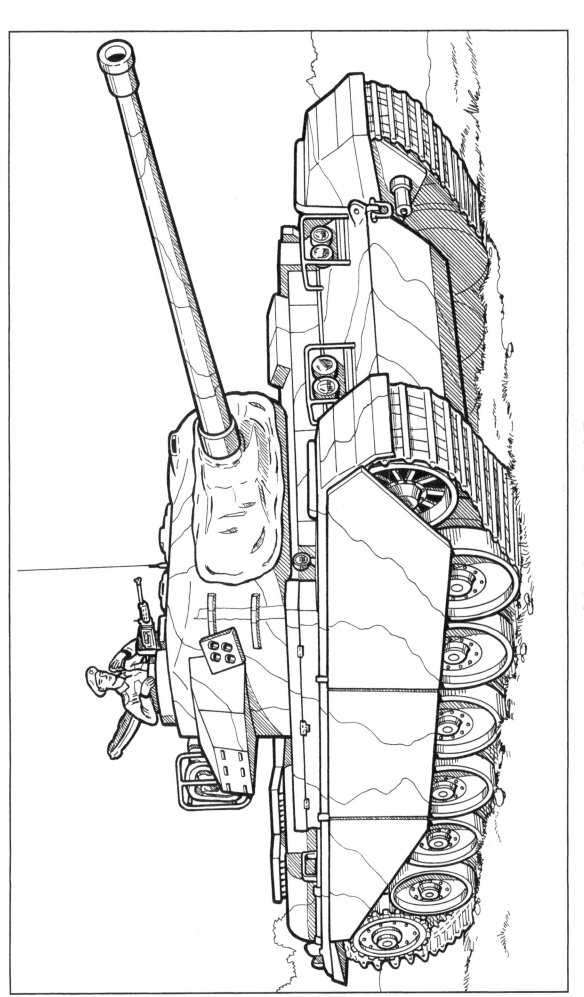

28. British A41 Centurion Main Battle Tank—1946

The British introduced the A41 Centurion main battle tank in 1946. It was well armored, equipped with a progressively larger caliber of main gun systems, and featured good road speed and mobility. The earliest versions mounted a 17-pounder (76-mm) cannon in the revolving turret. This was later upgraded to a 20-pounder (83-mm) gun, and eventually to its final armament of a potent 105-mm cannon. The Centurion was 32 feet long, 11 feet wide, and 9½ feet high. It was powered by a Rolls Royce V-12 gasoline engine generating 650 hp. With a weight of 113,792 lb., the tank could reach 27 mph and had a combat range of 120 miles. The crew of 4 armored, equipped with a progressively larger caliber of main gun systems, and fea- tankers was well protected by armor ranging in thickness from 2 to 6 inches. The Centurion was used in combat during the Korean conflict, the Vietnam War, and by the Israeli army with great effectiveness during their numerous battles with the sur- rounding Arab states. Centurion tanks were painted with either a tan and brown mottled camouflage design for Middle Eastern service, or with solid dark green or brown, black, and green camouflage patterns for European duty.

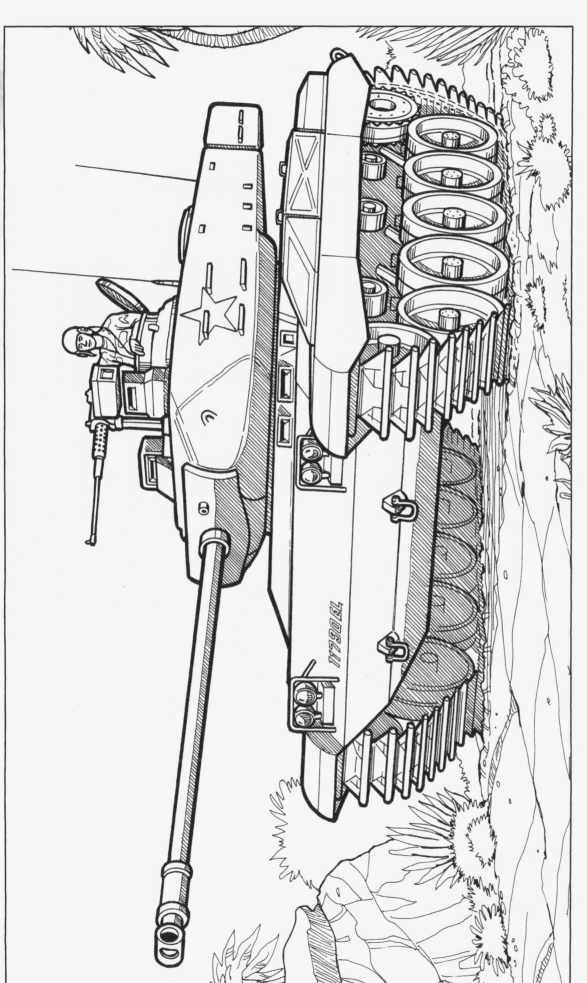

29. American M41 Walker Bulldog Light Tank—1951

The U.S. army introduced a fast, maneuverable light tank in 1951, the M41 Walker Bulldog tank. It was used very successfully in the Korean War. The Bulldog was powered by 500-hp 6-cylinder gasoline that could propel it to a speedy 44 mph. It carried a main gun of 76-mm caliber, as well as 2 additional machine guns. The Bulldog was 26½ feet long, 10½ feet wide, and 10 feet high. It carried a crew of 4, weighed 51,800 lb., and had an action range of 100 miles. The Bulldog was exported to serve in the armies of many nations including Taiwan, Brazil, Denmark, Chile, and Thailand. M41 tanks were usually painted standard U.S. army olive drab green.

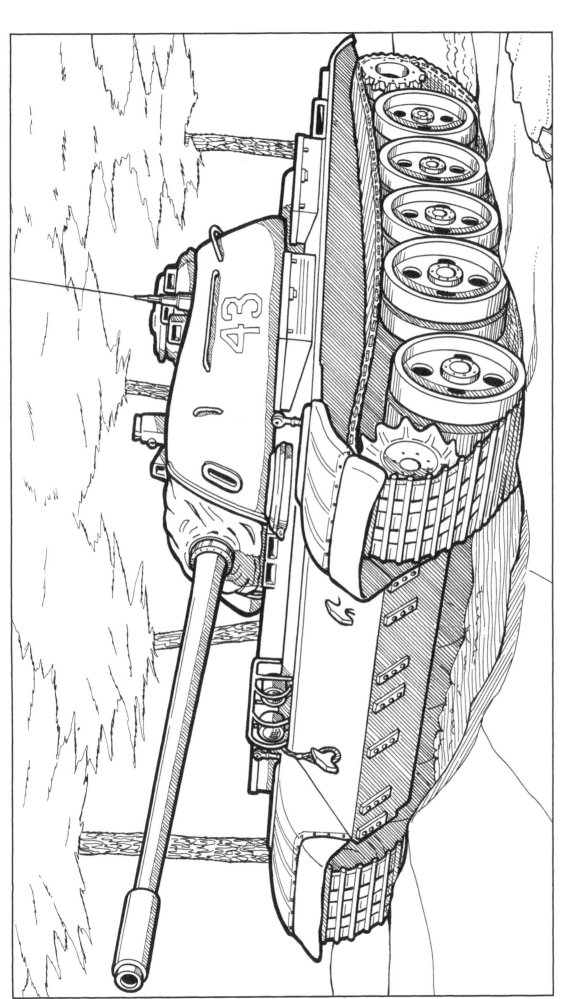

30. Russian T-54/55 Main Battle Tank—1949/1959

The T-54/55 series of main battle tanks served with the Soviet army and its Communist satellite allies during the cold war era. They also saw extensive combat in the Middle East with the armies of numerous Arab nations during their wars with Israel. The T-54 was introduced in 1949, and the T-55, an upgraded version with a more powerful engine, was brought into operation in 1959. It was during this era that the term "main battle tank" began to replace the designation heavy tank in the armored forces of the world. Both versions were armored with eight inches of steel around their rounded, bowl-shaped turrets. They carried a powerful 100-mm main gun, and two or three 7.62-mm machine guns. The T-54 was powered by a 520-hp V-12 diesel engine, while the T-55 had a 580-hp diesel engine. The 80,000-lb. vehicles could reach a road speed of 30 and 32 mph, respectively. They were 29 feet long, 10½ feet wide, 8 feet high, and had a substantial combat range of 300 miles. Produced in vast numbers by both the Soviet Union and Communist China, an estimated 57,000 T-54/55 series main battle tanks were built. In normal Russian army service, they were painted dark green.

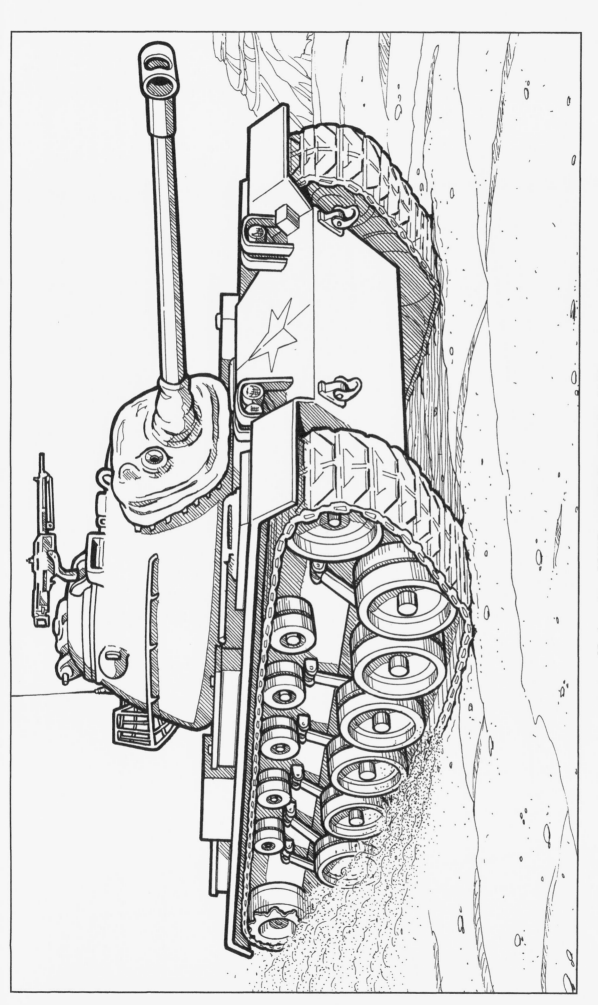

31. American M48 Patton Medium Tank—1952

The M48 Patton tank was an improved version of the earlier M47 Patton model which was rushed into production in 1950 for combat duty in the Korean War. Both vehicles were named for famed World War II American Army General George S. Patton, a brilliant tank warfare strategist. In its initial versions, the Patton was armed with a 90-mm main cannon. The last model, the M48A5, was upgunned with a more powerful 105-mm cannon. It is also equipped with a .30-caliber coaxial machine gun and a .50-caliber machine gun atop the turret. The Patton tank is protected by armor up to 4.75 inches thick. It is powered by a 12-cylinder diesel engine developing 750 hp. With this powerplant, the 103,488-lb. tank can reach a road speed of 30 mph and operate with a range of 288 miles. It is 28½ feet long, 12 feet wide, 10 feet high, and manned by a crew of 4 tankers. Most M48 Patton tanks were painted a standard olive drab color.

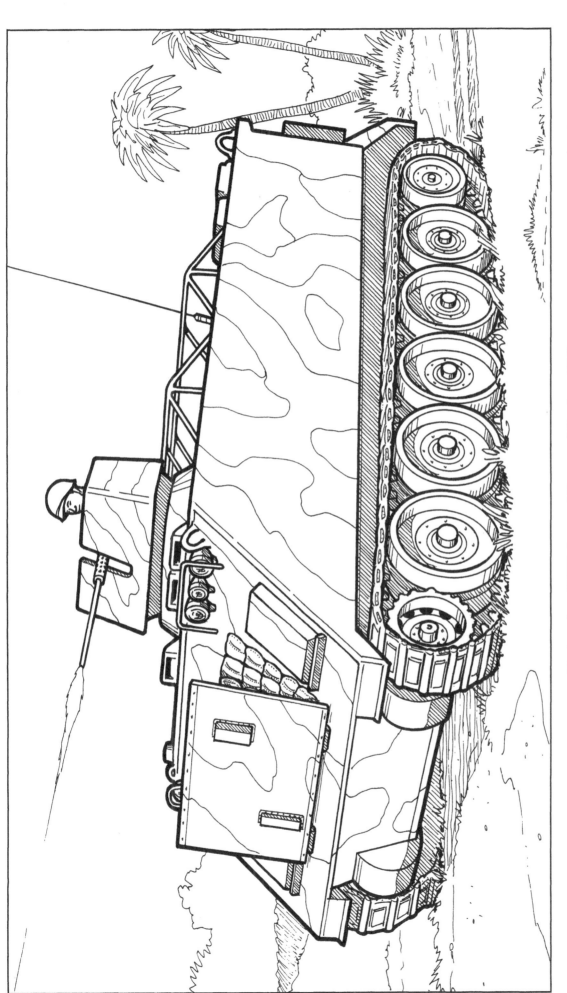

32. American M113 Armored Personnel Carrier—1961

The bulky squat shape of the M113 armored vehicle became a familiar sight to American television audiences during the 1960s and 70s, who viewed it on the nightly news as it disgorged American soldiers into battle in the jungles and rice paddies of Vietnam. The M113 performed a variety of functional tasks in the Vietnam War including troop transport, infantry fire support, mortar platform, flame-thrower, and anti-aircraft platform. Its most common usage was as an armored personnel carrier. In this configuration it was armed with up to 3 machine guns, both .30-caliber and .50-caliber. It was operated by a crew of 2 or 3, and could carry 11 fully equipped troops. It was 16 feet long, 8½ feet wide, and 8 feet high. With a weight of 24,950 lb., the M113 could reach a road speed of 42 mph powered by its 215-hp 6-cylinder diesel engine. It was protected by aluminum armor with an average thickness of 1.73 inches. Additional protection was afforded by a steel plate at the front of the vehicle that could be swung open to carry sandbags. They are still in active service with the U.S. army where they appear in standard army olive drab, or various mottled multicolor camouflage schemes.

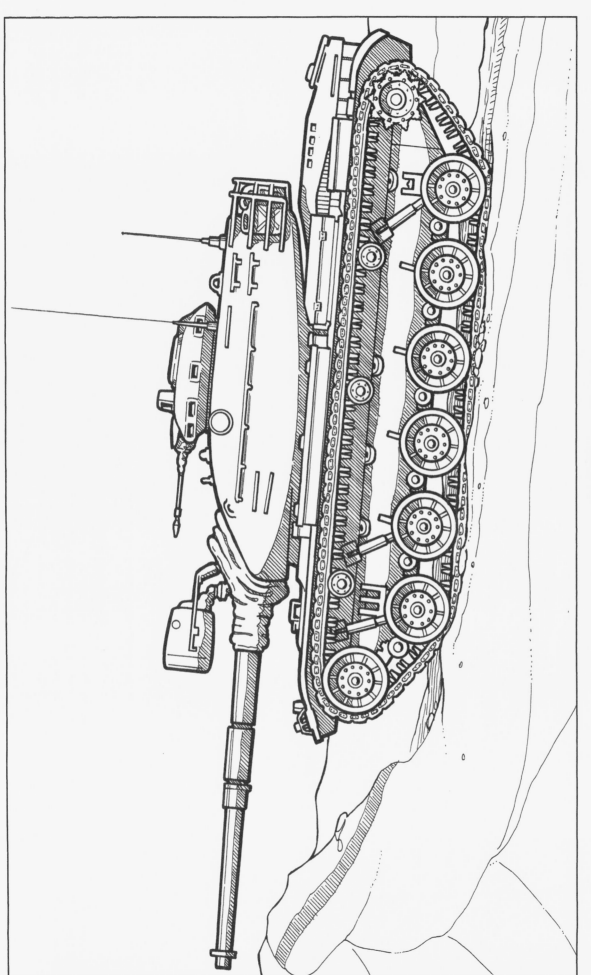

33. American M60A3 Main Battle Tank—1960

The premier American tank of the 1960s and 70s was the formidable M60 main battle tank. The successor to the M48 Patton, it has gone through a number of upgraded versions since 1960. The final model—the M60A3—is pictured above. It is armed with a 105-mm main gun, a coaxial .30-caliber machine gun, and a .50-caliber machine gun located in a rotating cupola atop the tanks turret. The M60 is protected by armor ranging in thickness from 1 to 5 inches. The M60 weighs 107,520 lb. and is powered by a 750-hp twelve-cylinder diesel engine. It has a road speed of 30 mph and a combat range of 300 miles. The tank is 31 feet long, 12 feet wide, and 10½ feet high. It is operated by a crew of 4 tankers. The latest model, the M60A3, features a laser rangefinder for its main gun and infrared thermal sights for night combat. It has been used very effectively by the Israeli army, and by the U.S. army and marines in the 1991 "Desert Storm" operation during the Persian Gulf War.

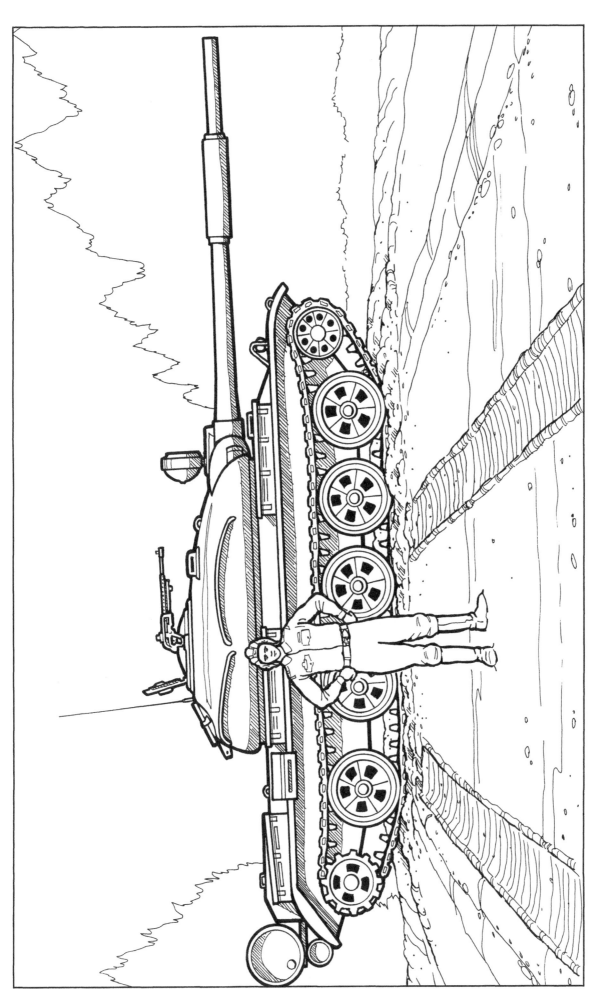

34. Russian T-62 Main Battle Tank—1963

The T-62 main battle tank was an upgraded version of the T-54/55 series. It served during the 1960s and 70s. It was fitted with a powerful 115-mm main gun and one 7.62-mm machine gun. The tank was 28½ feet long, 10 feet wide, and 7½ feet high. It carried a crew of 4 and weighed 87,808 lb. The T-62 was equipped with a 580-hp V-12 diesel engine, giving it a considerable road speed of 38 mph and range of 406 miles. The tank was protected by a layer of armor up to 9.52 inches thick. In the 1982 Arab-Israeli conflict, the T-62 was resoundingly defeated by the Israeli army using their formidable Merkava main battle tanks. In Middle East service the T-62 would appear in desert tan, and in European operations would be painted dark green.

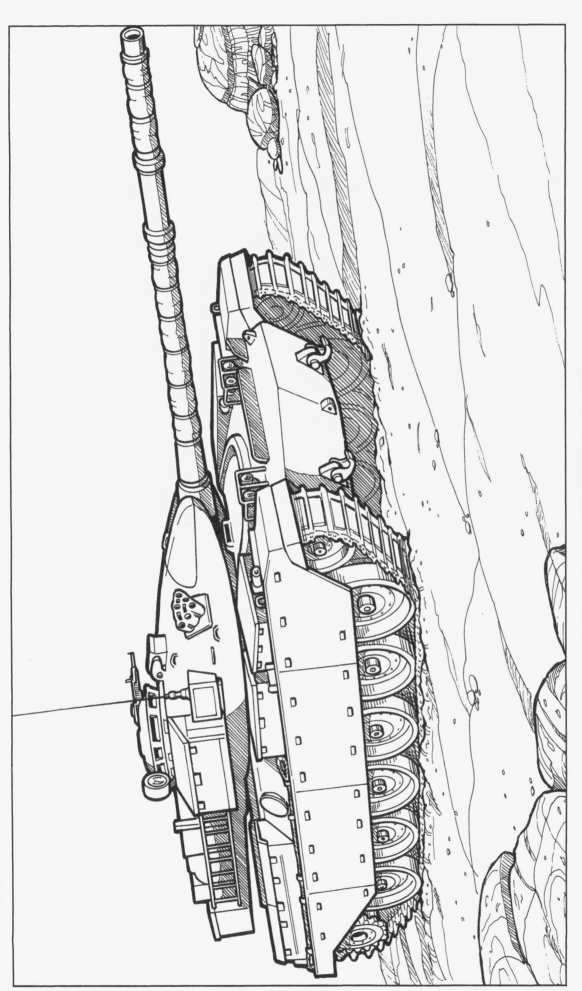

35. British Chieftain Main Battle Tank—1963

The powerful tank depicted above is the Chieftain, successor to Britain's very effective Centurion. The Chieftain was introduced into service in 1963 and still remains in operation with some British armored regiments. It is fitted with a potent 120-mm long-barreled main gun. As shown above, the gun barrel is fitted with a thermal sleeve to prevent deformation of the barrel from heat buildup as the gun is fired repeatedly. The tank is also armed with a 7.62-mm machine gun atop the turret. The Chieftain is protected by steel plate armor and an additional layer of Stillbrew laminate armor, the exact composition of which is classified. It is a large vehicle, with a length of 35½ feet, a width of 12 feet, and a height of 9½. It weighs a hefty 120,736 lb, with its crew of 4 tankers. It is driven by a 6-cylinder engine generating 750 hp, can reach a road speed of 30 mph, and covers a combat range of 310 miles. It is fitted with a laser rangefinder for the main gun and thermal-imaging optics for night combat. Chieftains are normally painted in a dark green-and-black mottled camouflage design.

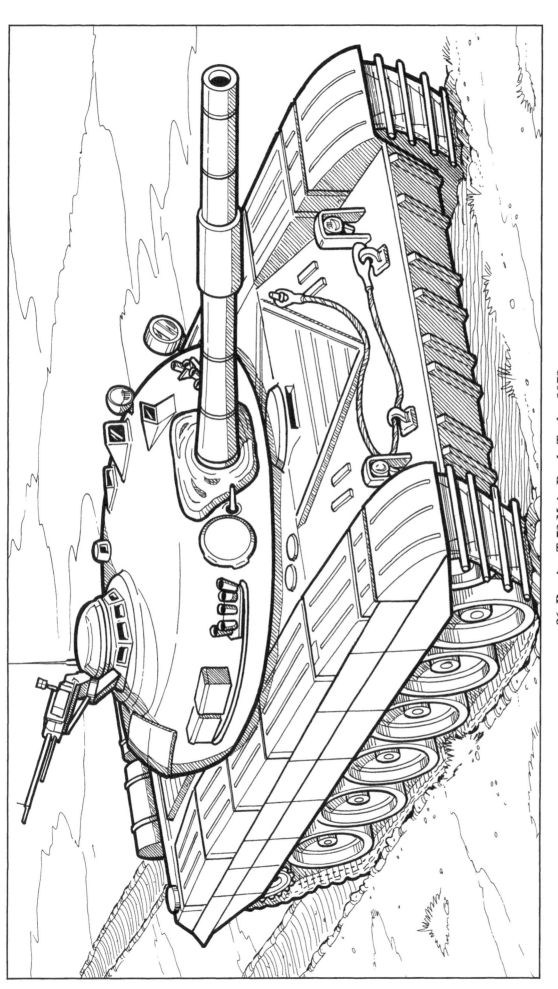

36. Russian T-72 Main Battle Tank—1973

The most widely operated Russian tank in current service is the T-72 main battle tank. In addition to the Russian armored forces, the T-72 is also used by Syria, Iraq, and Poland. An estimated 17,000 have been built since its introduction in 1973. It mounts the current leader in main gun caliber, an impressive 125-mm cannon. It is also equipped with a 7.62-mm coaxial machine gun and a 12.7-mm machine gun on the turret top. Precise information on its armor is classified, but it is believed to be 8 to 10 inches thick in critical areas. The T-72 has a V-12 diesel engine producing 840 hp. This can propel the 85,568-lb. vehicle to a cross-country speed of 40 mph. It is smaller than other contemporary main battle tanks, with a length of 30½ feet, a width of 15½ feet, and height of 7½. It carries a crew of only 3. Most modern tanks carry a 4-man crew: commander, gunner, gun-loader, and driver. The T-72's 125-mm main gun has an auto-load system, eliminating the gun-loader crewman. Despite its impressive main armament and thick armor, the T-72 did not fair well in combat. Israeli Merkavas knocked out dozens of T-72's in their battle with Syria, and American M60A3 and M1A1 main battle tanks destroyed hundreds of T-72's in the 1991 Persian Gulf War. The T-72 is gradually being replaced by the most modern Russian tank, the T-80 main battle tank. The T-72 is often painted in a dark green and dark gray irregular camouflage design.

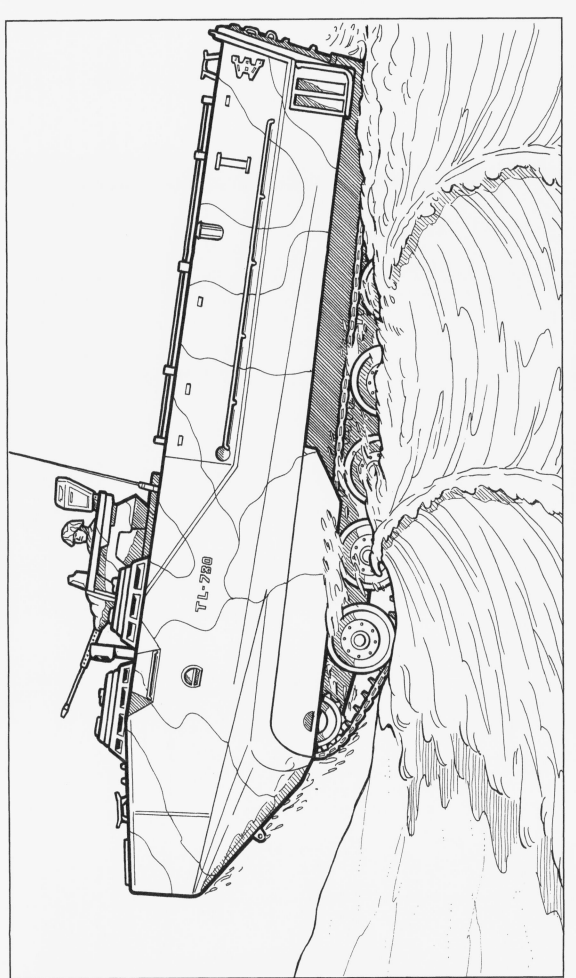

37. American LVTP-7 (AAV-7) Amphibious Assault Vehicle—1971

The United States Marine Corps specializes in seaborne amphibious landings for their troops and equipment from specialized assault ships anchored offshore. The marines proceed to land on the beaches using amphibious, tracked troop-carrying vehicles. The most widely used such vehicle today is the LVTP-7 pictured above. It is a large armored troop carrier, 26 feet long and weighing 50,241 lb. The LVTP-7 is 10 feet wide and 10 feet high, and carries a crew of 3, plus 25 fully equipped marines in the rear compartment. It can reach a water speed of 9 mph driven by water jets, and when on land, can travel at 45 mph propelled by its tracks. To power its drive systems, the LVTP-7 is fitted with a 400-hp diesel engine. It has an aluminum hull with armor protection 1.8 inches thick, and is armed with a .50-caliber machine gun in a rotating cupola atop the hull. In 1985, it was redesignated by the marine corps as the AAV-7. These amphibious assault vehicles are painted in a variety of camouflage colors including green, black, tan, and gray.

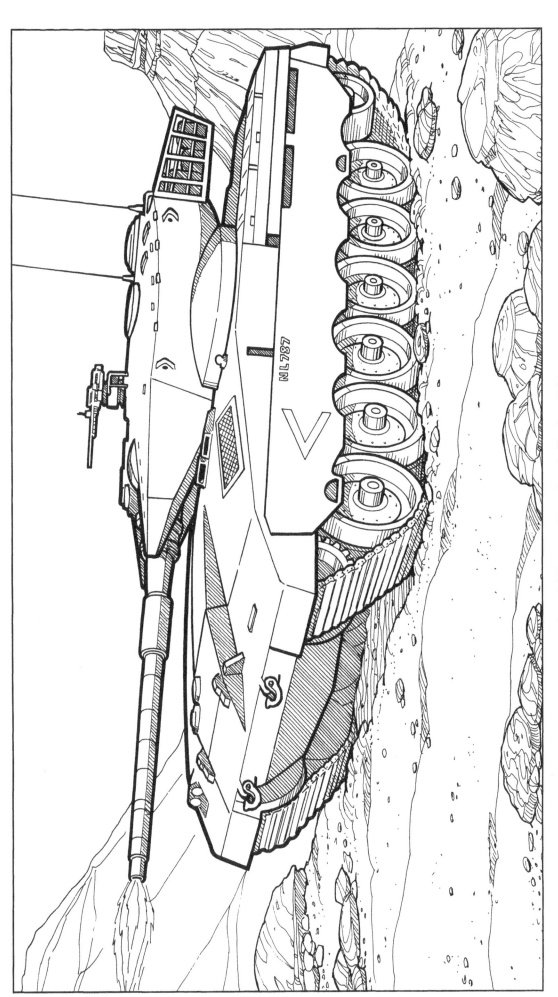

38. Israeli Merkava Main Battle Tank—1980

The tough and combat-proven armored fighting machine shown above is the Israeli Merkava (chariot) main battle tank. With Israel relying so heavily on its armored forces for protection against its hostile neighbors, they developed an extremely rugged and effective main battle tank. The Merkava was introduced in 1980, and first saw action against Syrian forces in 1982 when it decimated the Russian-made T-62 and T-72 tanks fielded against it. Crew survivability on the battlefield was the paramount feature built into the Merkava. The vehicle is heavily armored, and the exact specifications are kept top secret. The low silhouette and sharply angled facets of its turret make it a tough vehicle to target and hit. The initial version of the Merkava was armed with a 105-mm main gun. The latest model, the Merkava III, has been upgunned with a deadly 120-mm cannon. It also carries secondary armament of three 7.62-mm machine guns and one 60-mm mortar. Since armor protection and firepower were the primary requirements of the Merkava, it is somewhat slower and less maneuverable than other contemporary main battle tanks. The Merkava III is powered by a 1,500-hp diesel engine, giving it a maximum speed of 29 mph. The Merkavas weigh 122,976 lb., are 27½ feet long, 12½ feet wide, and have a height of 8½ feet. A 4-man crew operates the tank over a combat range of 310 miles. They are usually painted in desert tan camouflage.

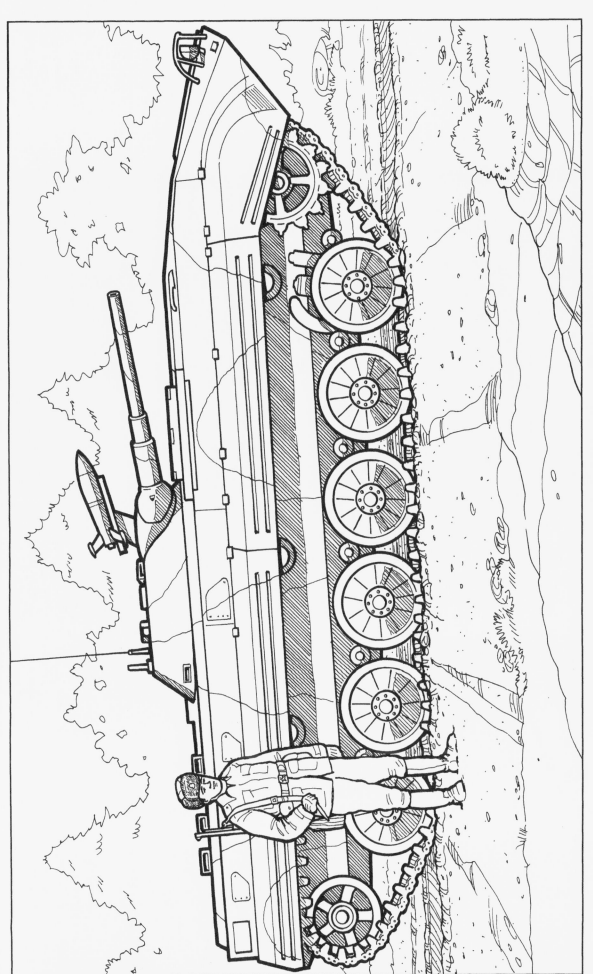

39. Russian BMP 1/BMP 2 Infantry Fighting Vehicle—1967/1982

The Russian armored forces deployed a fast-moving infantry fighting vehicle beginning in 1967. The BMP 1 is used for troop transport and reconnaissance. It has a crew of 3 and can carry 7 fully equipped soldiers. Within its low profile turret the BMP 1 mounts a 73-mm cannon and a coaxial 7.62-mm machine gun. It is also equipped with a turret-mounted Sagger anti-tank missile. The vehicle is powered by a 6-cylinder 300-hp diesel engine, giving it a top speed of 40 mph. The vehicle is 22 feet long, 10½ feet wide, 6½ feet high, and weighs 41,000 lb. In 1982, the BMP 2 was brought into service. It is armed with a longer range, high velocity 30-mm automatic cannon, and a more accurate Spandrel anti-tank missile. BMP's usually appear painted in dark green or dark gray.

40. German Leopard 2 Main Battle Tank—1979

The Leopard 1 and 2 series of main battle tanks began service with West Germany in the mid-1960s. The Leopard 2 entered service in 1979 and is the current main battle tank of the German armored forces. It is armed with a powerful 120-mm main cannon, one coaxial 7.62-mm machine gun, and one 7.62-mm machine gun atop the turret. The Leopard 2 is protected by a heavy thickness of multi-layered armor (whose composition is top secret), making the tank extremely difficult to destroy.

Despite its weight of 120,960 lb., the Leopard can reach a road speed of 45 mph, making it one of the fastest tanks in the world. Its powerplant is a 1,500-hp 12-cylinder diesel engine. The vehicle is 31½ feet long, 12 feet wide, and 9 feet high. It carries a crew of 4 tankers and can operate within a 310-mile range. Leopard tanks are painted dark green, or in a mix of dark green and dark gray mottled camouflage patterns.

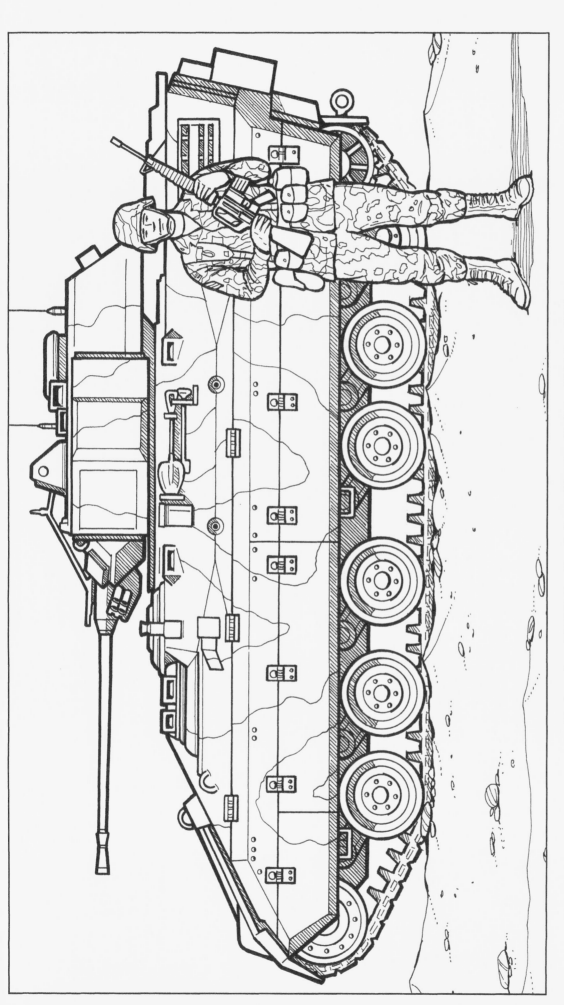

41. American M2/M3 Bradley Infantry/Cavalry Fighting Vehicle—1981

The M2 Bradley fighting vehicle received its "baptism under fire" during the 1991 Persian Gulf War, Operation Desert Storm. Used for troop transport, infantry fire support, and fast-scouting missions, there are 2 versions of the M2: the infantry fighting vehicle, and the cavalry fighting vehicle. The main difference is that the infantry version carries a crew of 3 and 7 fully equipped troops, while the cavalry model carries a crew of 5 and a heavier ammunition load. The Bradley is armed with a rapid-fire 25-mm cannon, a coaxially mounted 7.62-mm machine gun, and 2 tube-launched, optically-tracked, wire-guided (TOW) anti-tank missile launchers located on the side of the turret. It normally carries a complement of 10 TOW anti-tank missiles. With its 500-hp 8-cylinder diesel engine, the Bradley has a top speed of 41 mph. The vehicle is covered by a classified type of aluminum and laminate armor. It can also be equipped with additional bolt-on reactive armor. It is 21 feet long, 10½ feet wide, 9 feet high, and weighs 49,865 lb. The Bradley is painted either solid olive drab, solid desert tan, or in a variety of camouflage designs incorporating tan, brown, green, and black irregular splotches.

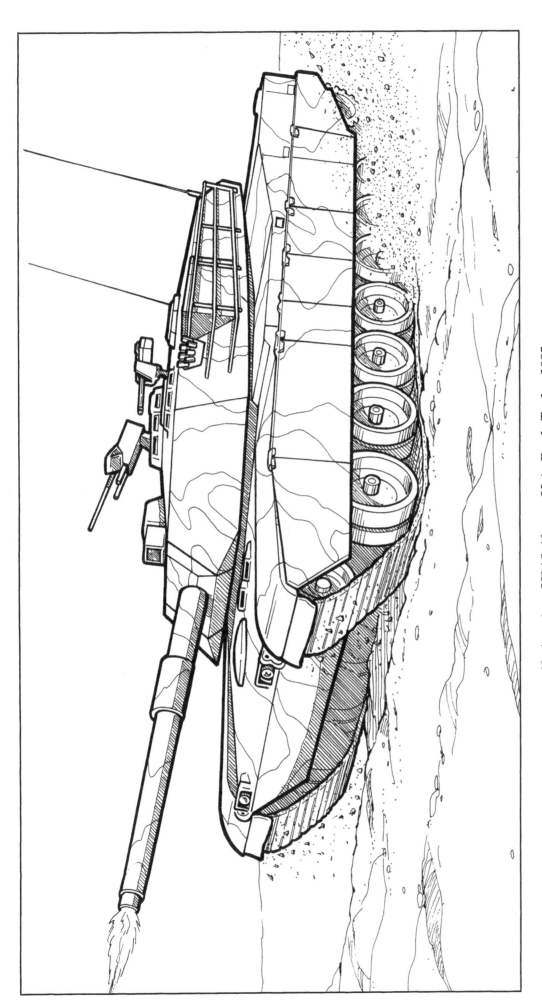

42. American M1A1 Abrams Main Battle Tank—1985

The armored divisions of the U.S. army are equipped with the finest main battle tank in the world—the formidable M1A1 Abrams. It was combat-tested in the deserts of Iraq and Kuwait during the Persian Gulf War. The M1A1 destroyed hundreds of enemy tanks and other armored vehicles without a single Abrams tank being knocked out! Such a stunning victory was attained through courageous and highly motivated tank crews, and superior American technology embodied by the tank's special features. The vehicles' gun system is the most deadly weapon ever carried by an armored fighting vehicle. The 120-mm cannon features a computerized fire-control system with a gun stabilization mechanism that allows the weapon to be fired with great accuracy while the tank is moving at high speed. It is equipped with a laser rangefinder and sophisticated night vision optics. The Abrams is also armed with a coaxial .30-caliber machine gun, a turret-mounted .30-caliber machine gun for the gun-loader, and a turret-mounted .50-caliber machine gun for the tank commander. The tanks' heavy armor protection is composed of a top-secret multi-layered combination of steel, ceramic, and classified materials. The M1A1's turret is additionally designed with sharply angled facets to deflect enemy shells. The vehicle is powered by a gas turbine engine developing a tremendous 1,500 hp. Although the Abrams weighs in at a hefty 126,000 lb., it can attain a rapid cross-country speed of 45 mph. The M1A1 is 32 feet long, 12 feet wide, and 9½ feet high. M1A1 tanks are painted in camouflage schemes of dark green, dark brown, and black for European duty, and a mix of tan-and-brown irregular patterns for desert operations.

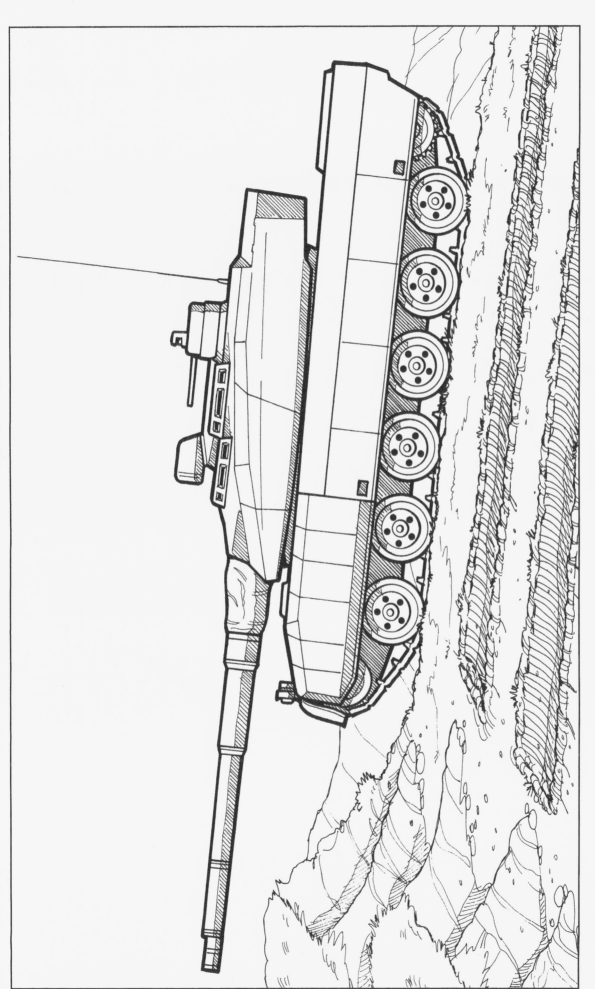

43. French Leclerc Main Battle Tank—1992

The current main battle tank fielded by French armored forces is the Leclerc. It was brought into operational service in 1992. It is an advanced design with heavy armor and firepower. The Leclerc's main weapon is a 120-mm cannon with an auto-load system. This feature, along with a remote-controlled turret-top machine gun, reduces the tank's crew to 3 members. The Leclerc's armor protection is classified, but believed to be a combination of metal/laminate and explosive reactive armor. Despite being a very large vehicle, the Leclerc has a road speed of 45 mph, very fast for its weight of 117,700 lb. It is powered by an 8-cylinder diesel engine generating 1,500 hp. The tank is 30 feet long, 11½ feet wide, and 10 feet high. The French military normally paints their armored vehicles in a solid dark green color.

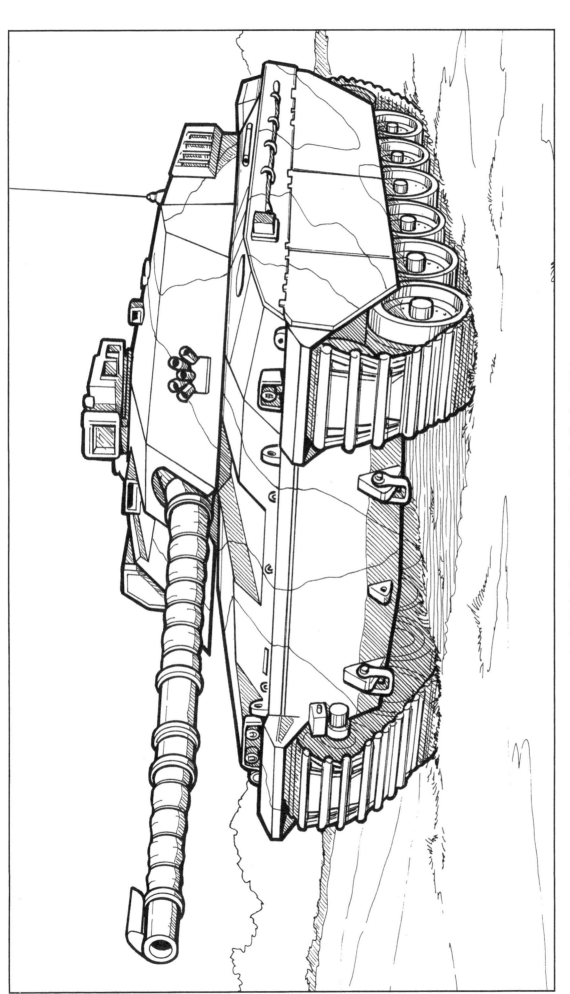

44. British Challenger 2 Main Battle Tank—1994

With the long British military tradition associated with tanks, including the machine's invention, it is only fitting that the United Kingdom currently produces an extremely capable series of main battle tank known as the Challengers. The Challenger 1 was introduced in 1982, and its successor, the Challenger 2, was brought into service in 1994. The Challengers mount a deadly 120-mm main cannon equipped with advanced features, including computerized gun stabilization, laser rangefinders, and night vision devices. Their secondary armament consists of two 7.62-mm machine guns. The Challengers' armor protection is perhaps the best in the world.

It is comprised of ultra-secret Chobham armor (named after the facility where it was devised), a composite of metal, ceramic, and other materials resistant to both heat and penetration. This exotic substance makes the tank almost impervious to armor-piercing enemy shell-fire. The Challenger is a large vehicle, 38 feet long, 8 feet wide, and 10½ feet high, weighing a massive 137,500 lb. Powered by a Rolls Royce diesel engine producing 1,200 hp, the heavy Challenger has a top speed of 35 mph. Challengers can be seen in desert tan, dark green, or camouflage patterns of dark gray, light gray, and dark green.